Preparing the perfect CV

Preparing the perfect CV

How to make a great impression
and get the job you want

5th edition

Rebecca Corfield

KOGAN
PAGE

20 14001 485

For YB

Publisher's note
Every possible effort has been made to ensure that the information contained in this book is accurate at the time of going to press, and the publishers and author cannot accept responsibility for any errors or omissions, however caused. No responsibility for loss or damage occasioned to any person acting, or refraining from action, as a result of the material in this publication can be accepted by the editor, the publisher or the author.

First published in 1990 by Kogan Page Limited as *Preparing Your Own CV*
Second edition 1999
Third edition 2003
Fourth edition published in 2007 as *Preparing the Perfect CV*
Reprinted 2007
Fifth edition 2010

120 Pentonville Road
London N1 9JN
United Kingdom
www.koganpage.com

ISBN 978 0 7494 5654 2

British Library Cataloguing-in-Publication Data

A CIP record for this book is available from the British Library.

Typeset by Saxon Graphics Ltd, Derby
Printed and bound in India by Replika Press Pvt Ltd

Contents

Look on our website for supporting downloadable CVs
that can be adapted for personal use.

To access, go to
www.koganpage.com/PreparingThePerfectCV
and enter the password: CV1347

Introduction

The world of work is changing fast. Many more of us will take temporary positions, have periods when we work on a freelance basis and move permanent jobs more often. Our careers are likely to change direction more than once in a lifetime of 40 years of working life. Job flexibility can mean job insecurity for some of us, forcing us to leave jobs before we want to, as employers' needs change and working roles are redefined. As a result, most of us will change careers and move in and out of different jobs many times in our working lives, perhaps going on training courses in between to make ourselves more employable.

This means that we are all applying for jobs more frequently in an increasingly competitive environment. Job-search skills that we used to need only at the start of a long period with one employer now need to be regularly sharpened and practised. The way that we present ourselves is crucial to being successful in today's job market. Every aspect of contact with a prospective employer needs to be as good as we can make it in order to impress.

Imagine this situation – you are looking to change your job when you notice an advert in the paper that seems right up your street. You are keen to put in an application until you realize that the advert specifies that you must send in your curriculum vitae or CV – and you do not have one. What's more, you have never had such a document and are not sure exactly what it would look like.

The fact that you are reading this book is likely to mean that you are:

▦ reconsidering your future if you have just been made redundant or had your hours reduced;

▦ looking for a job – perhaps you have been out of work for a while or have just finished a training scheme;

▦ trying to change your job – you may not be enjoying your current role or just feel that, for your career development, it is time to move on for some reason;

▦ planning a future change of career – while your job may be proceeding well at the moment, you may want to get ready for your next move in advance;

▦ preparing your personal job-search materials – even if there is no immediate prospect of a job change you may feel that it is sensible to keep your documents up to date just in case. You may want to check the current conventions and layout of CVs if you have not updated yours for some time;

▦ advising people in one of the above situations – you may be a careers or personal adviser, a teacher or a parent, wanting to keep your information about good practice current;

▦ interested in re-doing your CV; you have one but think it needs a 'makeover' to refresh and improve it for today's use.

You know that the paper processes of applying for jobs are what make the difference in terms of attracting the right kind of attention from recruiters. The key to getting an interview rests on impressing an employer in writing in most cases. You have heard that a curriculum vitae or CV may help to get the job of your choice and need help to know where to start.

The importance of a good CV

Feeling that you are in the wrong career or that you cannot get the job you want can be very depressing. Finding a job, or a better job, is fraught with difficulties at the best of times. Having to present yourself in a positive light when you are probably feeling overwhelmed, demoralized and not at your most self-confident may seem just too challenging. Even the most successful careerist can be anxious when it comes to applying for new jobs. You need the right help to compile a CV that will give you a big advantage in overcoming the hurdle of this lack of confidence that can affect any of us.

Anything that aids you in your job search is valuable but a good CV can be a real boon. A curriculum vitae is an extremely versatile document and it can enhance your job prospects regardless of your circumstances. You will benefit from compiling a curriculum vitae whether you have:

■ many qualifications or none;

■ had many jobs, or never worked;

■ been unemployed for long periods;

■ experienced career success or have not yet found your niche;

■ excellent references or none.

When an employer is looking for an employee, one of the applicants has to be successful. That person could be you – as long as your CV stands out from the rest as being full of evidence that you are the best candidate for the job. Equally important, if this evidence is presented in a concise and attractive way, your CV can be a powerful influence working for you. Your CV does not have to knock all the others off the employer's desk; it just has to be up there amongst the most impressive so that you get called in for an interview for the post.

Employers want an easy time when they are looking for suitable candidates to employ. If they can spot a good potential employee from the papers that arrive in response to a vacancy, they will spend much less time than usual in finding the right person for the job. Generally the numbers of people applying for every vacancy mean that any typically busy recruiters are looking for a way of reducing the number of CVs in front of them. Any that are less impressive, not as well presented or in some way disappointing, will be eagerly seized on – and thrown in the bin. This book shows you how to ensure that this does not happen to your CV.

However, there is an even more important reason for having your CV well prepared. Feeling in a position to apply for any job that takes your fancy or being ready to submit an application for a position that you hear of by chance, means that you are in control. It may sound like a small aspect of your life – it is one that is only represented by a couple of sheets of typed paper, after all. However, if you think of the significance of being confident of your ability to represent yourself at any time, in a manner of which you can be proud, you can perhaps see how an impressive CV under your belt can just be the tip of the iceberg.

Sometimes life can knock us off course, events can be bewildering and being able to choose a career rather than just being able to find a job, any job, looks like an optimistic dream. Taking this small step to equip yourself with the best possible CV could be just the start of you gaining more confidence in your own ability to affect your future across the range of activities in your life. It is an assertive, self-confident, forward-looking act that could lead to lots of other changes in your life. Let's get started.

How to get the most out of this book

This book was written to guide you in your first steps towards putting together a curriculum vitae or CV for yourself – even if you have never heard the words before. Everything about the document will be explained for you. You do not need to be an expert at getting jobs, a high-flier or someone who is good at 'selling yourself' to other people. The curriculum vitae will do that for you.

Examples of job adverts

We offer a competitive salary, an enjoyable work environment, and benefits such as company discounts, concert tickets, and contributory pension scheme.

Please write with career details to

Margaret Smith
Recruitment & Training Officer
VP UK Limited
1 Oxford Street
London W1V 6HE

PA-GROUP OFFICE ADMINISTRATOR based in PETERBOROUGH

We are the international headquarters for a new market-driven company, involved in the development and distribution of highly innovative home products.

The job: PA to our Chief Executive with UK and international responsibilities.

You are: Articulate and practical. You have excellent keyboard and other administrative abilities. You have good communication skills and can be part of a happy, ambitious team.

We offer: An excellent starting salary (£30,500, pension, medical insurance and generous performance bonus).

Please send your CV to: Mr Marcus Smith, Group Operations Manager, Aspen Lifestyle Products Ltd, Aspen House, Horsefair, Porterham PE1 5BQ.

Having the right CV is just part of the larger operation of finding a job – and that can be like playing a game. Several factors can help you to win in this game, and having a nicely written and presented CV is the place to start. Employers know roughly what type of person they are looking for, and you have to: (a) work out what they want; and then (b) convince them that you fit that description and are the candidate with the most to offer.

These advertisements are typical of those seen every day. You will find job adverts in Jobcentres Plus, employment agencies and newspapers, and on the internet.

Although the first advert asks for 'career details' to be sent, this is usually done by sending a CV and a covering letter.

To apply for vacancies like these you need to have your own impressive CV ready to send off straight away. Once you have read through this book and used the practical advice to compile your own CV, you will have started to take more control over your role in job hunting, and the next steps will not seem so difficult.

Chapter 1 explains exactly what a CV is and shows what a standard layout looks like. In Chapter 2 we examine how to put the document to the best use. The most perfect of CVs is no good unless sent to the right places and targeted at the appropriate jobs. We study the content of a good CV in Chapter 3, detailing exactly what to include and what to leave out for the best effect. In Chapter 4 we look at how it should be physically presented for maximum impact.

In Chapter 5 you can look at a selection of real examples of other people's documents. This will enable you to learn from their best efforts before you start on your own CV. Different styles are illustrated and discussed here. Chapter 6 draws together all the information and gives you a step-by-step guide to compiling your own effective curriculum vitae. Chapter 7 indicates where you can find CV help on the internet. You will find helpful dos and don'ts at the end of each chapter, and points to remember are highlighted as you work your way through the book.

1

What is a CV?

A CV is an outline, normally on paper, of a person's educational and professional history. This may sound as though it should only be used by 'professionals' or those with high-level qualifications, but *everyone* can benefit from having a well-written and well-presented CV when job hunting. It is a simple and accessible way of introducing yourself to potential employers and can be a vital tool in obtaining the chance to impress them face-to-face at an interview. Many employers and employment agencies will expect you to have your own CV ready and up to date. Many vacancies can be applied for by sending in your CV online.

What does a CV look like?

Every CV will look different, and that is the way it should be. Like the real 'story of your life', it will be different from every other person's story, for each of us is unique. Typed on to paper, it is usually two to three pages long, printed on one side of the paper only. Black ink and white paper are most commonly used.

What does curriculum vitae mean?

The words come from the Latin and mean literally 'the course of your life' or the brief story of your career. The term is often abbreviated to CV, and these two letters are used to represent the term in this book. In some countries a CV is known as a résumé (pronounced 'rez-ume-ay'). This is a French word which means 'summary'.

Therefore, given the individual nature of this document, there is no such thing as the *right* way to construct a CV. Every careers adviser has different ideas about the best way to design and fill in the document. Every employer will like to see this style or that layout. Each thinks that this or that should be included, in this or that manner. This book outlines the way I have found employers to be most impressed, and uses three basic rules that you will find repeated throughout the book:

1. Keep it simple. An uncluttered document gets read before a fussy one. Plain layout of your document will help the reader to see how much you have to offer.

2. Make it clear. Direct language and straightforward sentences are easy to read and understand.

3. Keep it short. Less is often more when it comes to a CV.

In fact these rules should be applied to any written document, but are particularly important in a CV where only simple, clear and brief documents will be taken seriously.

What is in a CV?

Standard CVs are usually split into a maximum of seven different sections:

1. *Personal details:*
   Includes name, address, telephone numbers, e-mail address, nationality, etc. These are the facts about you and explain how to contact you.

2. *Education:*
   Provides dates, names and locations of schools and colleges attended and details of any qualifications that you may have obtained. This section also outlines the subjects that you have studied. It is usually written in chronological order – earliest first.

3. *Employment:*
   Specifies dates, employers' names and locations, job title and main activities/achievements of each position held. It is normal to begin with your current or most recent job.

4. *Other skills:*
   Covers your other practical abilities or education, including training courses and other subjects studied, eg languages and computer skills.

5. *Interests:*
   Includes hobbies, sport and leisure activities.

6. *Additional information:*
   Details other skills or type of work wanted. This section contains your statement about the contribution you can make and what kind of person you are. It can also include any specific achievements and successes you have had.

7. *References:*
   Names, addresses and full contact details of two people who will provide character references for you.

How do you start to write a CV?

Welcome to the world of CV writing. If you have not approached this task before, you are about to discover the benefits of having such an aid to help you with your career development. Many people are worried about how to write this document. You may be someone who has been putting off writing your own CV, believing that it would be tricky or too demanding. You may even have not applied for vacancies if they asked for your CV because you did not know how to compile one. It is true that you will need to commit a certain amount of time and effort to the job, but you stand to gain a very valuable tool.

Writing a CV for yourself is time-consuming and laborious, but certainly worth the effort. The way to start is to read through this short book in order to understand the basics of compiling a CV. Then you can begin working through your own career history, guided by the examples contained in the book. If you concentrate on just one section at a time you will soon find that the whole document is fairly straightforward to complete.

It would be much simpler if there were CVs in this book that you could just copy, but unfortunately, because each person has different experiences and skills, your CV *has* to be completely original, and individual to you alone. Although different CVs may look similar, each one will contain unique material.

Obviously, you can learn from other people and on pages 61–115 in Chapter 5 you will find many different examples of the way that CVs look once they have been put together. At the end of Chapter 6 on page 131, a blank form has been included for you to use when you start compiling a version for yourself.

The finished product will aim to:

- highlight the good points of your experience and skills. This means portraying what you have done and what you know in the best possible way;

- play down any weaknesses in your history. This means minimizing any less successful times and covering up any gaps;

- portray your career as consistent and show clearly what you have to offer.

How long should a CV be?

Most CVs should be limited to just two sheets of A4 paper or three at the very most, so this document will not take you too long to write, once you know where to start and have help in presenting the information correctly.

When your CV is finished you will be able to update it regularly as you add to your experience and skills. The effort will be worthwhile and your confidence in presenting yourself to potential employers will grow when you see how impressive your history can look, once it has been well thought out and displayed.

Sometimes there may be justification for a slightly longer document but this only happens occasionally. Some examples could be:

■ you have had many different jobs and have worked for many years;

■ you are in the entertainment business with many different appearances to list, or in a creative or academic role with productions or written work to describe;

■ you have travelled extensively with your work, eg with the armed services.

Dos and don'ts

✔ Do see writing your CV as a worthwhile and rewarding task.

✔ Do look at as many other people's CVs as you can for inspiration.

✔ Do think about the kind of impression you want to convey to employers.

✔ Do spend time thinking about the skills and qualities that are seen as valuable for the kind of position you are looking for.

✔ Do spend some time looking at job adverts in your field to see specifically what employers are asking for.

✗ Don't think of this as a chore – make up your mind to enjoy creating your CV.

✗ Don't reinvent the wheel – use good examples that you see in other CVs.

✗ Don't be too honest! We are aiming to minimize weaker areas and promote your good points.

✗ Don't hesitate! Get going on your first draft right now.

✗ Don't worry if there are some bits of information missing at this stage. You can fill in the gaps later on.

Points to remember

1. Understanding the point of a CV will help you get inspired to get going.

2. You will see many different styles of CV; you need to find one that you feel comfortable with.

3. Stick to the simple headings recommended here in your CV, so that it appears uncluttered, rather than adding many more of your own.

4. Even if you don't need a CV right now, it is always a good idea to have an up-to-date one for your own reference.

5. Creating a job file for all relevant pieces of information will pay dividends when you start to write your CV.

2

What is a CV used for?

A CV is a very flexible document and can be used for many different purposes. Here are just some examples of when a CV may be used:

- Applying for advertised vacancies when the employer specifies that applicants must send in a CV – see the examples on pages 61–115. Employers want all applicants to submit similar documents in order to simplify sifting and short-listing. They will then be able to compare and contrast the strengths and attributes of the different candidates by checking through the CVs that arrive in the post.

- Applying for vacancies in a speculative manner, or 'on spec'. This is when you write off to companies in the hope that they may have vacancies, now or in the future. If there are no current vacancies you can ask them to keep your name on file. Your CV can be a lasting record of your details for the company to refer to in case of employment opportunities in the future. You can find companies' names and addresses in newspapers, trade and telephone directories or on the internet.

- By employment agencies or Jobcentres Plus when they are putting your name forward to the employers on their books. An agency may gather a handful of the most appropriate CVs to submit to an employer in the hope that one will be selected as right for the post.

▨ As an *aide-mémoire*, or memory-jogger, when you are completing application forms. All the information about your history will be included in this document, and this will save you from having to remember all the dates and information each time you have a different form to fill in.

▨ For general business purposes, when self-employed or doing consultancy work, etc. Your CV can act as a brief biography, outlining your experience and skills for any contract work that may require a bid from you.

▨ As an introduction to companies or banks when you need to explain your background for some purpose. CVs are not only of use when you are applying for work. Your finished document can serve as a summary of your background for other occasions.

▨ When making an application to a college for a course of study or training. Decisions about college places, particularly for mature candidates, may rest on how appropriate your background and experience have been for the subject to be studied. Your CV can help explain these aspects of your career to an admissions tutor.

How can a CV enhance your job prospects?

Have you ever seen a job that looked interesting, but have not applied for it because it asked you to send in your CV and you did not have one prepared? By the time the job is advertised, it is too late to draw up a CV from scratch, and this can make you feel that you are unable to apply. This situation need never arise again.

Many jobs that are advertised in newspapers are filled very quickly indeed. If you can rush your CV to the company concerned, your application stands as good a chance as that of anyone else. However, if you are really keen on a job, it is no good dashing off a CV at the last minute. Hasty work will not match up to the best of the competition. An impressive CV needs time and care to compile.

Be prepared

Once you have produced a CV that you are pleased with, you have one big advantage over many other job-seekers: you are ready to apply for a job whenever a suitable one comes up. Instead of flying into a panic at the thought of having to prepare all your details, you will be ready to send off your personal introduction to the employer promptly.

Another great advantage of having an impressive CV to hand is that similar information can be sent to any number of different employers; the only information you need to change is the covering letter that is sent with it. Your CV will be deliberately designed to be suitable for many different situations.

How do you start to compile an effective CV?

Working on a CV of which you are really proud can take a long time. The finished document can be improved on and altered continually, even when you are ready to use it.

Making sure that you are including the right information is a time-consuming business initially. All your details need to be listed, and then you must be ruthless in weeding out any unnecessary information. A short CV is the only finished product that will be read.

Your CV will last your whole career long. It will change and develop as you do, but once written will provide the template that you can adapt as your experience grows and the requirements of the job market change. When the CV is looked at in this light, you can appreciate that it is going to be a very useful investment of your time, effort and writing ability to construct the best document you can.

You need to think of putting your CV together as though you were starting a major project at work or college. To do it properly you need to devote the necessary resources to it and take the task seriously:

▓ Get yourself mentally prepared. Enlist the help of family and friends by letting them know that you are embarking on this task and that it may take you some time.

▓ Treat it as work. This is not an activity to cram into odd minutes and spare moments. You will be preparing a well-written document that will last over the years, so take it seriously by ensuring that you have adequate time to devote to the task.

▓ Think about where and how you will do it. You need a quiet time and adequate space to:

 – sit and work;
 – think and concentrate in a creative manner;
 – collect source materials and deal with paperwork;
 – use a computer;
 – use the telephone if you need to talk to other people;
 – research different employers;
 – print and edit documents;
 – file documents and store finished copies.

The hardest part is getting started. Once you have begun you will want to complete it all.

To start with, you will need to spend time collating the details of all the jobs you have done in the past, as well as the facts of your educational career. This may mean rooting around in old diaries or records and asking family members for their help. Certificates from school or college can provide useful education details and pay slips may tell you about the dates of jobs. Looking back through old photographs can sometimes help to jog your memory if you are stuck on exactly which dates are the correct ones. You may not want to include every piece of evidence in the final version, but collecting everything together enables you to make clearer choices about what to keep in. One important point to bear in mind is that you want to be able to use the finished CV for more than one application, on more than one occasion.

The importance of presentation

Once you are happy with the content, the correct presentation of the document can be as challenging a task to attend to. A good CV will speak volumes about the sort of person you are. If you have taken the time to sort out the document properly, you will appear well organized and thorough (useful in any job), and if the CV is well presented, you will look as though you are a person who is careful about details and confident at the same time.

Presentation covers more than just the look of the document; it also relates to the way you include and order your material. Otherwise good CVs can be ruined by inconsistent layout and illogical order. Your content needs to be organized to make it easy for the reader to follow. It is irritating to have to keep mentally jumping around when reading a CV that repeats information and does not follow on in a sensible layout. It also often means that the CV is longer than it needs to be.

A CV is never used on its own, and will always be accompanied by a covering letter (see the examples at the end of Chapter 6 from page 125). This letter is your opportunity to be specific about exactly how you fit the particular job that you are applying for, picking out the relevant skills, qualifications or experience that you have detailed in your CV.

Stressing your good points

Writing the CV is excellent practice in being assertive about yourself and your achievements. Most people are hopelessly bad at putting their best points forward. We are all more used to being shy and quiet about our assets. But each one of us is unique and has our own history, strengths and ambitions, and those that relate to you can shine out from your completed CV.

Job applications require you to be positive about everything you have been through so far, whether it be many different jobs, all for a short period, being out of work or bringing up children away from the paid work market.

This means that an added benefit of preparing your CV is that it helps to get you into the right state of mind to go all out for the job you want. It encourages you to think positively about what you have to offer and can act as your launching pad into the job market.

Minimizing your weaknesses

Sometimes there will be aspects of your career history that you are not happy about. Although it would be wrong to be untruthful about your details, there are ways of accentuating those things of which you *are* proud, to take the attention away from anything else. This means that you maximize your achievements and minimize the rest. As we work through the different sections of the CV in the next chapter, looking at what information to include, we will consider ways of handling problem cases.

Even the most successful high-fliers will have some disappointments or embarrassments at some point in their career path. The trick is not to emphasize these but to shine the spotlight instead on those aspects that enhance your potential and of which you are most proud.

Reflecting on your career

Writing a CV for yourself may well lead you to reflect on your career path to date, whether you want to or not! Almost inevitably, you will find that the process of pulling together details of all your academic study, your work experience, your interests, achievements and abilities, provokes some self-analysis. You can't help but relive some of those experiences as you include them, and you may find you start to make links and draw conclusions about yourself in the process.

Listing your progress through study and work can make you feel, at best, proud and glad; at worst, neutral and undecided, or frustrated and disappointed. You could be prompted to reflect on what makes you happiest and most fulfilled in work. It could be that you are missing some things that you used to enjoy, or that you wish you could be moving in a different direction. You could notice what has prompted you to move jobs or change aspects of your career in the past. You could make connections between successes in work or study and the rest of your life.

Often your CV will confirm your sense of self, of who you are, and of the interesting and impressive aspects of your career. Sometimes writing a CV can make you decide to make a different future for yourself instead of carrying on, or it can just confirm the choices that you are making right now. It may be a stimulus to go back to studying to improve your qualifications to move to another level, or to downsize your work to give you a more balanced life. Either way, using your CV as a prompt for some clear thinking about the way you are living your life is part and parcel of the process. That is as it should be, for this is not just another document; it is the story of your life.

Dos and don'ts

✔ Do get organized – it will help you prepare a better document in the long run.

✔ Do keep working on different drafts of your document until you are happy with it – this could mean three or four tries.

✔ Do keep positive. You need to feel upbeat in order to sell yourself in your CV.

✔ Do try to see your CV as an employer would when reading it.

✔ Do keep checking that what you are writing is clear, simple and easy to read.

✗ Don't underestimate the time you will need, especially if this is your first attempt.

✗ Don't start writing straight away – do some thinking and planning first about how you want it to look.

✗ Don't get demoralized about the work involved. Think of all the people who have CVs; they will all have had to go through this process at some stage.

✗ Don't get bogged down in the details. Move on to the next section if you need to.

✗ Don't guess at spelling and grammar. Use a spellchecker and look up difficult words in a dictionary.

Points to remember

1. Turning the TV off and using quiet, soothing music may help you to get going.

2. Thinking as widely as you can at the start will help you cover everything that you want to include.

3. Working for hours can make you stale; keep having a break every 20 minutes or so to keep your concentration at its peak.

4. If you get fed up and stuck, leave it alone, let some time elapse and then come back to it afresh.

5. Getting others to look at what you have written can provide a valuable, different viewpoint.

The content of your CV

We are going to look at the content of your CV in this chapter, and in the next chapter at the way it looks. What you put into your CV is important and there are some crucial things *not* to do. Understanding what puts the reader off can help us in putting together a better CV.

Here are some of the most common errors made in compiling a CV.

The most common CV content mistakes

- The CV is too long. Aim for two pages, three at the very most.

- It is dull to read. It needs to have impact as well as being informative.

- Playing down what you have to offer instead of making the most of it.

- Missing out the significant skills and experience gained.

- Just sticking to the facts and not describing personality or character.

- Including too many details about past jobs, instead of just the key points and achievements.

▨ Using the past tense instead of the present tense. Active 'doing' words are much more interesting and immediate to read.

What should be included?

So how do you start to put together your own CV? This chapter looks at *what* information to use, and Chapter 4 contains advice about *how* to present the information in the best way.

What you put into your CV is crucial to the way that it is perceived by the reader. This chapter outlines the main elements of a typical CV, and we will consider all the sections in turn in order to see what should and should not be included in each.

Remember the three important points mentioned in Chapter 1:

▨ Keep it simple.

▨ Make it clear.

▨ Keep it short.

Although there is no single right way to compile a CV, the method described in this book is a tried and tested way of constructing a good CV for yourself.

Even if you have never seen a CV before, you can use common sense to think about what a document like this needs to contain. For a start it must include identifying personal details as well as the facts about how and where you can be contacted. You will need to share your educational background and include your work history too. Describing your hobbies, interests and any other skills that you have can help to make your CV come alive. Referees' details will help any employer who may want to check you out in advance of meeting you.

The greatest challenge is to include information that describes the kind of person you are. Many employers are looking for a good 'fit' between applicants and the team in which they would be working. It is very difficult to glean from a list of schools, colleges and jobs what character someone has. To make your CV properly realistic, we need to transform these two pages of typing into a living, breathing representation of the whole you. You will be shown how to achieve this task later in this chapter.

If you are at the stage where you want to start compiling your own document, think broadly about what you could put into each section as it is described below. Make a note of anything that could be included in your own CV as you read on. You can always cut the material back before you produce the finished version. This is much easier than having to add elements later.

Getting started

Now it is time for you to commence work on your CV. It can feel difficult to begin, but immediately seems easier once you get started. So get going at once, either writing by hand on a big blank sheet of paper or direct on to a computer. As you read about what is needed under each heading in this chapter, complete the details for yourself. The CV will not write itself but once you have embarked on the task, you are halfway there.

Making your CV stand out

At the stage when your CV arrives on the employer's desk, he or she knows nothing more about you than the information that you are going to reveal in your CV. This means that you have a responsibility to do yourself justice, by explaining easily and simply who you are, and what you have done so far. You are an interesting and valuable person and your CV is the means by which you convey this to an employer.

The one way to ensure that your CV is noticed by an employer is to make it very obvious if you have done anything at all unusual. If you have travelled on a school or college trip, been involved with any voluntary groups or in different sporting activities, make sure you include these points.

You may be noticed by the employer just because there is something different about your CV which makes it stand out from all the others. If you can describe some activity that other people will not have taken part in, you will appear to have had different experiences from those of others, and therefore, to an employer, you may seem to be more worth meeting at an interview.

At this point, all we are trying to do is to find out what material *could* be put into your CV. The amount of information that you compile may well end up being cut down a great deal, but that stage will come later on in this book.

Taking each section in turn, let us look at the CV for Patricia Mary Sharp, as an example. Patricia starts with the first section of her CV, which contains her personal details. Most people start here as it contains information that you should have easily to hand.

1. Personal details

This section is usually not too difficult to compile, as it is just about the factual details of your life. Name, address, telephone number and e-mail address are put at the beginning of the CV so that your name and the way to contact you cannot be overlooked. Always include an e-mail address if you have one. This is the easiest way for an interested employer to get in touch with you.

Name:
Names are written as:

Patricia SHARP.

Middle names are unnecessary as they will only confuse the reader, and how often do you ever use yours? The surname (or family name) should come at the end. This order of names makes more sense than Sharp Patricia, as this is not the way her name is normally used. We do not use P M Sharp either, as initials will also be difficult for an employer to understand and remember.

If you have more than one name (for instance married women who also use their maiden name), make sure you use the name that you would want to be called if you were employed as a result of the CV.

As some names can be unusual, it helps to put your second (or family name) in capital letters, so that it can be easily identified.

Address:

Always use your full address and postcode. If you do not have a secure or permanent place to live, find an address that you can use for correspondence. Perhaps a friend or family member would let you use their address so that you can receive mail in a secure place where it can easily be retrieved regularly.

Telephone number:

Always include your telephone number if you have one. An interested employer may just want to pick up the phone and talk to you. If you are not on the telephone, try to find a friend or relative whose number you could use, so that messages could be taken on your behalf – as long as you are sure that they will be taken reliably.

Put the full STD code and number, eg:

020 7928 0000 *or* Oxford (01865) 000000

to be as clear as possible.

Only include a work contact number if you are certain that it will not matter if a potential employer calls you there. Most people would not want their present employer to know that they have been applying for other jobs.

Include your mobile number if you can be contacted on that.

E-mail:
Include your e-mail address if you have one. For many employers, it will be more convenient to contact you this way.

Date of birth:
Recent government legislation has outlawed discrimination by employers on the grounds of age. This means that you do not need to put your age or date of birth on your CV – and it will be positively helpful for employers if you leave them out, because they can look at your CV without taking your age into account. Of course, the dates when you attended school and college may give rough pointers to your age, but this is acceptable practice. If you are applying for something where age is an important consideration, such as a course only available to a certain age group, or for an apprenticeship with a cut-off upper age, or for certain roles in the armed forces, it may be sensible to include your date of birth.

Nationality:
For some jobs, this aspect of your personal details is very important. If you are from another country, it is essential for you to specify that you are able to work here, eg:

Nigerian (with full UK work permit).

Refugee status is also worth mentioning, eg:

Ethiopian (with refugee status in the UK).

On the basis of keeping the information as simple as possible, some personal details which are not worth including are:

health, height, weight, place of birth or country of birth,

unless you have reason to think that including one of these factors in your CV would increase your chances of getting the job. Examples could be if you were born in the place where the company is based, or if the job particularly requires a certain physical standard, such as a minimum height requirement.

Some people include a recent head-and-shoulders photograph with their CV. Attaching a photograph is common in some countries. This can attract attention to your CV and get you noticed, but in the UK it is not normally done. The exception is for jobs where your physical appearance is relevant, perhaps in the entertainment industry. I was recruiting for a job and only one person out of nearly 100 included a photo with her CV. It just made her application look very odd compared with those of other people. When we go for an interview we try to look as good as we can, but sending in a photo can make it appear as if you think the only important requirement is what you look like. Don't risk being the odd one out – let your words on the page do the talking and leave the picture out.

2. Education

This section is for you to outline your educational history from secondary school onwards. The further away this time is from the present, the less relevant the information will be. So, for instance, recent school leavers will give full details of all the subjects they studied in this section, as they will have less, or perhaps no information to put in the employment history section. More information on presenting a CV for a school leaver is included with the example on pages 61–115 in Chapter 5. If you left school and college many years ago and have been on more recent and relevant company or professional training courses, it may be worthwhile including them here. You may then want to retitle this section 'Education and Training' instead.

The information needed is, first, the dates that you attended your secondary school (from age 11 onwards) – either just the years, or the months and years. Next, the name and location of the school(s) should be included, although the whole address is not necessary. You may have changed school frequently, in which case just list the last one. To locate a school, just the town and county or the city and postcode are appropriate. The last pieces of information required are any examinations passed or, if none were taken, the subjects studied. You do not need to put down the details if you failed an exam – your intention is to stress strengths and minimize weaknesses. However, you may decide to list 'subjects studied' for those where you either did not take or pass an exam, so that you get credit for the work you did. If you obtained distinctions, prizes or scholarships in certain subjects, include this information as it will set you apart from other candidates. If you worked on any particular projects, list these as well.

College details should be given in the same way. To use our example again, Patricia Sharp includes the following information:

2002– 2007	Swansmead School Birmingham B14	**GCSEs:** English language Mathematics, History Science, CDT
2007– 2009	Bishops Technical College Wolverhampton	**BTEC National Diploma:** Business Studies

As you can see from this example, school experience is usually written chronologically, with your first school coming at the top of the list and then other periods of study listed in order, finishing with the most recent. This is so that employers can check that you have the basic qualifications needed before looking at your later exams and courses taken. College life offers more variety than the school experience in terms of courses or modules followed, learning opportunities and style of study undertaken. Give full details explaining what your college experience was like. If you were engaged in any extra-curricular activities such as belonging to clubs or societies that linked in with your studies, make a note of them here.

Typical problems

'My school career was a disappointment but I have studied and succeeded in my jobs since then. How can I make this late development look good?'

If you have attained vocational qualifications rather than academic ones, retitle your Education section 'Education and Training' and list your professional courses there. Give full details of all the things you have learnt about. Use the 'Additional information' section (see page 37) to talk about how you have gained a lot from your post-school studies, explaining that training linked to work is especially rewarding and meaningful for you.

3. Employment

This section covers the different jobs that you have done. The information required is very similar to the last section on your educational details. You need to research all the starting and finishing dates of all the different jobs you have done, including part-time, vacation and voluntary jobs, especially if you have not had much employment experience. If you have only just left school, you could include any work experience here.

Either just the year, or the month and year, is again appropriate for each position. If you are older and have had many jobs, or have had gaps between jobs that you would like to 'smooth over', then just the year may be appropriate.

For this section, the order of your employment history is reversed. Starting with your most recent job, you list them all and end up with your first employment. The reason for this is so that the job in which you had the most responsibility, normally your last, comes first. You don't need either the full address or postcode here; see the example below.

2006–2009	Perkins Confectioners London SW15	Clerical Assistant: Using Word and Excel, invoicing, dealing with customers, filing, telephone work, keeping petty cash.

The main difference between this section and the last is that here we need to say what the job title was in each case, and to specify the main duties for each different job.

You can see that only the main duties are listed, and they are written in note form. Also, they all begin with a verb: using, invoicing, dealing with, filing, keeping petty cash, etc. To write full sentences would take up too much room. Although similar, this part of your CV is more difficult to complete than the last. You have to consider not only what to include but also how to describe the things that you have done in your work history. Most jobs involve many activities. You cannot list every single thing you did during years in one job but you need to do justice to the variety of key tasks that you undertook. These tasks represent what you learnt in the last job, and describing them enables you to demonstrate that you have these skills. It may well be that similar skills will be needed in the post for which you are now applying, and the employer needs to know that your experience is transferable to the new position.

These 'transferable skills' are crucial in the CV. You are trying to show employers that you can do the job that they are advertising. If you have done the same or similar tasks before, that provides proof of your ability. Even if you have not worked in exactly the same role before, but you have carried out broadly similar activities, then you will be able to make a contribution. Many employers will look for these transferable skills when they are shortlisting for a position. They search CVs for key words or phrases that they have already identified as being significant. For instance, a project management role might be sifted by including only those CVs that include some or all of the following: management, team leader, systems, IT skills, work processes, timelines, etc.

Here is a list of words that could be useful to give you ideas about how to describe the work you have done in previous places of employment:

achieving
adapting
administering
advising
advocating
analysing
assessing
challenging
changing
checking
choosing
coaching
communicating
compiling
conducting
co-ordinating
creating
deciding
delegating
delivering
designing
developing
diagnosing
discussing
enabling
engineering
establishing
evaluating
facilitating
formulating
guiding

helping
initiating
inputting
launching
leading
liaising
managing
mentoring
modernizing
monitoring
negotiating
organizing
participating
performing
persuading
planning
preparing
problem solving
producing
providing
recruiting
regulating
representing
researching
securing
selecting
selling
serving
shaping
supervising
training

Read through the list to see if the words apply to roles you have played in any of your previous jobs. There are many more active verbs than those used here but this list may inspire you to think of others that help to describe your work experience. Using positive and active words like these contributes to creating a powerful impression of a strong candidate. Your words on the page are all that readers of your CV have to go on, in terms of their perception of you. The more you can encourage their view to be of a dynamic and high-achieving candidate, the better your chances of being invited to an interview.

Here are some more examples to show you how well these can turn out.

2002–2006	Advertising Executive: Responsible for running administration in the advertising section; liaising with advertising and PR companies, organizing placing of adverts and promotions in different titles; developing office IT system for both Apple Macs and PCs; representing the company at the Frankfurt Book Fair.

2000–2007	Supervisor: Managing group of seven; setting and monitoring budgets; planning production schedules and evaluating output; motivating staff and developing team working; achieved internal gold standard award for high performance for three years running.

2003–2007	Manager/Partner: Owner and manager of 50-seat floating restaurant, employing and supervising staff, setting up and monitoring systems, managing stock and sales, co-ordinating press and customer relations.

2005–2008	Administration Co-ordinator: Organizing car rental services across Europe, trouble-shooting, establishing and monitoring new client packages, dealing with European sales managers.

2006– 2008	Sales Assistant: Serving customers; organizing displays; dealing with problems; tidying stock; attending to health and safety matters; handling cash; participating in training and team meetings; developing my sales expertise.

If you have recently left school or college and do not have much, or any, work experience to put in this section, you need to think hard about what else you could use. If you have had any school or college work experience placements, this is a useful substitute. Voluntary activities can be very helpful as they can provide the experience that employers are looking for. If you really have no experience at all of any kind of work, you need to fill that gap straight away. Contact your local volunteer centre for opportunities for you to contribute to a local charity or voluntary organization. There is something for everyone to do, and you will be able to find some way of helping others that ties in with your interests. You may also be able to gain a job reference if you keep volunteering for some time.

Employers will be interested in the Employment section of your CV for the following reasons:

▪ to see if you have skills that are transferable to the job on offer;

▪ to check that you are able to work in a disciplined and structured environment;

▪ to look at the range and type of experience you have gained.

If the type of employment is not clear from the name of the company where you have worked, and it is relevant to the job that you did, it is worth putting it in brackets after the name, eg:

Simpkins   **Clerk**
(Solicitors)

Before you start to write up your own details, try to think of all the things that you did in each job, and list them all. Even though it may seem obvious to you that a clerical assistant would do some filing, it may not be clear to anyone who has not done exactly the same job before, and it may be just what the employer is looking for evidence of. Think through everything you did in each job, from the activities that occupied you when you started the job to those you were engaged in at the end.

The idea of a CV is that your history will be seen in date order. Remember, if you have had many large gaps in your employment history, you may find it more useful to put just the year of starting and finishing a job so that the end of each job merges more into the beginning of the next.

If you were in charge of other people in a job, make sure that you mention this at the beginning of your duties, and also include any promotions that you received during your time in the job. Were you involved with any special projects in any of your jobs? Did you sit on any working groups or take part in specific committees that added to your work role? Describe them in this part of your CV.

Did you play any significant role in any of your jobs? Do you have achievements that you can claim as yours or in which you played a part? You can portray these here to enhance your job details and to differentiate you from other applicants.

If you have had many different jobs, remember that the important fact is what sort of person you are now, and what skills and experience you have acquired to date. Jobs from further back may show your breadth of experience, but in that case they can be grouped together, such as:

'I have worked in many different types of employment during vacations, including shop, office and factory work'

or:

'I have four years of pay-roll and accounts work with agencies throughout the Birmingham area.'

I do not recommend including details either about why you left each job, or about what salary/wages you earned in each position. If the employer wishes to find out these things, they can be discussed in a subsequent interview.

4. Other skills

Include in this section any other skills that you have learnt that you would like an employer to know about. Examples could be familiarity with computer packages such as word processing, databases or spreadsheets; first aid; full, clean driving licence; basic or advanced language ability.

Don't be tempted to undersell yourself here. If you can speak a language but not write it, then say 'Fluent in spoken Spanish' rather than 'Basic Spanish'. Most employers will be attracted more by spoken ability that you could use with their clients, customers or suppliers. Rack your brains to think of other practical skills that you have learnt over the years. Include any courses or training that you have undertaken that do not sit easily anywhere else.

5. Interests

Your interests can help to show that you have a well-rounded personality and do not live for work alone. Any interests that you have or have had in the past which are out of the ordinary will help you to stand out.

I would not recommend being too specific about any political or religious interests unless they are of direct relevance to the position that you are applying for. To make sure that you do not prejudice your chances, it is better to say that you are actively involved in the local community – the reader of your CV may hold different views from your own. It is best to steer well away from any issue that has an opposing point of view in your CV. The topic in which you believe passionately may be very off-putting to the person selecting which candidates to shortlist. Some people find it hard to believe this. They think that because they spend every spare moment campaigning for green issues, donkey sanctuaries, their particular religious belief or an end to global poverty, the rest of the world is bound to be impressed.

Be assured that there is no political, religious or campaigning issue on this earth that does not have equally vociferous and zealous opponents. It could be that the employer reading your CV is one of them. Even if this person doesn't have strong views either way, he or she may look askance at someone who does, thinking that a diehard campaigner could be a disruptive influence in the workplace. Don't risk losing your chance of an interview through revealing too much of your private beliefs if they have nothing to do with the job at hand. Keep your private activities just that – private.

Try to put down some physical activities, as well as some cultural ones, to show that you are a healthy, active and lively person. Try to move beyond just listing your selected pastimes. If you can add something about your main interests, you will enable the reader to see how they fit into your life and therefore help them to bring your CV to life. Note-form is all you need here, eg:

'Karate – member of a local training club; travel – I have visited most major European cities; pottery – this has developed from an evening class into a major interest and I have now exhibited several pieces locally; swimming, walking and cinema.'

You do not actually have to spend time on *all* these activities at the moment, but be sure that you know enough to talk about every interest you list at the interview. Employers often pick on your hobbies as an easy area of questioning. In this example, they may want to know what style of karate you studied. Not an easy question to answer if the nearest you ever got to karate was watching a martial arts film, and the employer is a black belt!

If you belong to any clubs, societies or professional bodies, you can mention them here. Remember that an employer will be interested in any activity that makes your document stand out from the crowd of CVs that he or she is considering.

When making the decision about what information to include in this section, always remember that the point of putting down your hobbies is to show the reader that you are a well-rounded and balanced person, with a satisfactory life of your own outside work.

Try to avoid the most obvious interests, which we all share. This means that 'reading, socializing and watching TV' should not be included unless you read specific types of books or watch certain programmes, not just soap operas and the news.

6. Additional information or personal profile

With many CVs to consider, employers are looking for more than just the minimum skills and experience necessary to be able to do the job. They want people who will fit in the company or organization properly. Therefore to get to the next stage of the recruitment process and be invited to an interview, your CV must also describe the sort of person you are. After all, you and I could have attended the same school or college and worked in the same places but we would still be completely different people.

To find material to use in this section, write a list of 10 words or short phrases that describe your good points. The words in the list may be those that have been used about you in references or appraisals in the past, or compliments that have been paid to you when you have made a valuable contribution at work. Perhaps you were praised by a line manager or supervisor. What specific words did they use? They should describe some aspect of your personality rather than things you know how to do. The idea is to gather positive words that help portray your character at its best. Some words apply to just about all of us, so try not to include very obvious ones such as 'punctual', 'friendly' or 'sociable' in your 10.

Here is one person's list as an illustration:

■ motivated;

■ calm;

■ polite;

■ loyal;

■ thorough;

■ hardworking;

■ serious-minded;

■ accurate;

■ determined;

■ a good team worker.

The list itself won't appear on your CV, but we can turn it into a useful description of your character, which can be included. Once you have compiled your list, pick the six or seven most relevant points to the kind of job you are likely to apply for. For each of the words or phrases, construct a sentence about yourself, where possible giving an example of when you have demonstrated that kind of behaviour, and in this way work up a short passage about your personality.

From the list above, the result follows:

'I am a hardworking and loyal person. My experience working in shops has taught me that a polite and calm approach to caring for the customer works best. I try always to be accurate in my work and take a pride in being thorough about details. I enjoy working as part of a team.'

Here is the list of a completely different character:

■ energetic;

■ determined;

■ keen to win;

- persuasive;
- ambitious;
- talkative;
- good sense of humour;
- creative;
- hardworking;
- quick learner.

The resulting paragraph from this list could be:

'My sales training built on my persuasive skills and natural determination. I learn quickly and my good sense of humour helps to lighten the atmosphere in any team when deadlines approach. I try to be creative in any task and work hard to contribute with energy and ambition to agreed team goals.'

Now compose your own list and paragraph. Write your list here:

1. ....
2. ....
3. ....
4. ....
5. ....
6. ....
7. ....
8. ....
9. ....
10. ....

The result may sound as though you are blowing your own trumpet too much but please resist the temptation to include negative points or to qualify what you write as in 'fairly good', 'quite accurate' or 'usually hardworking'. Plain, positive words are needed here to allow your strengths to shine out of your CV. All other job applicants will be portraying themselves in the best light possible, so do not hold back. This section is normally written out in full sentences. Now turn your 10 words into a description of yourself:

....

....

....

....

....

....

This section can be very important for those with gaps in the other sections of their CV. For instance, if you have brought up children and have therefore been out of paid work for some time, this is the place to explain the gap in your career. An example of this type of CV is included in Chapter 5, on pages 91–93.

If you have travelled for a time, you can write about it here. If you are changing career direction, this section is your chance to explain why you are interested in the new type of work.

Here are several examples of the type of information that could be included.

> 'For the last seven years I have been looking after my two children. This experience, coupled with my previous job, has taught me how to budget and plan, keep to deadlines, organize work schedules, work as part of a team and delegate tasks.'

'I am mature, very adaptable and can work cheerfully under pressure. I am painstaking in my work, honest, punctual and trustworthy. I make friends easily and enjoy working as part of a team.'

'I have many years' experience as a finisher in the clothing industry. After bringing up my family, I am eager to return to full-time employment and use my expert skills to contribute to an effective team. I can offer reliability, punctuality, stability and commitment.'

'During the past few years, I have spent a lot of time doing voluntary work in the community, both here and abroad, helping to provide for the needs of others. This has given me a sense of perspective, developed my people skills and enhanced my ability to manage projects on time and to budget.'

'I have extensive experience in designing, writing and testing programs, and versatile knowledge of software and operating systems. As well as these technical skills, I can communicate well with users, to explain, train and problem-solve for them.'

'I have a disciplined and organized approach towards my work, as well as being dependable, self-motivated and flexible. I am well-presented and am an asset to any company I work for. My skills are highly transferable to any aspect of publishing.'

'I help to make things happen and am always reliable and enjoy moving projects forward. I am a confident, focused and well-motivated person. I combine an approachable appearance with the ability to empathize with others. I have strong convictions and am prepared to challenge when necessary. However, I take pride in being independent and objective in my consideration of issues, and entrepreneurial and innovative in my analysis.'

'I am a proficient organizer and experienced manager of projects and staff teams. Financial and resource management have been central requirements of my work. I maximize team efforts and motivation, which are critical to successful delivery, and in addition I provide leadership where necessary. I lead by example, enabling others to develop confidence in their own abilities.'

'Following three GCSEs, I achieved academic success after 20 years outside education with an MA in Marketing, linking communicating with campaigning. I see myself as a change agent, modernizing and adapting structures, and assessing and helping to deliver changes. I was able to concentrate on succession planning, spotting potential stars on the staff, developing, nurturing and fast-tracking future Regional Officers.'

'I combine management experience at the sharp end of training with an understanding of the private sector and a readiness to take on the responsibility for organizational strategy at all levels. The centre I run began in 2000 as a good idea that needed fostering and developing. I have provided a clear vision of its future and effective team direction, and today it is a flourishing success story. My enthusiasm, calm approach to problem solving and commitment to the highest professional standards ensure quality of provision for clients and value for money for project partners.'

This additional information part of your CV is sometimes called a 'personal profile'. There are different ways of approaching the layout of this section and these will be covered in the next two chapters when we look at how to present your CV.

You can see from these examples that there are many different ways of describing yourself and a variety of writing styles in which to do so. The nature of the CV is that it is personal to you in terms of what you put in it and how you lay it out. Employers will be looking for candidates who seem to fit with their type of employment. Don't leave to chance whether you make the grade or not. Study the details of the company or kind of sector you are interested in. Find out the way that they write about themselves. Model your prose on what you find. Try and use words that chime with what you have researched so that they will be interested in calling you for interview. If the company literature talks about 'a jackets-off team' and 'lively, go-getting staff', then make sure you write about yourself as being full of initiative and convey the impression of an energetic person who will let nothing get in your way.

If the firm deals with detail and accuracy, think through how you can stress your thoughtful approach to your work and let it be known how you have received credit in the past for being painstaking and having particularly high standards.

7. References

You should name here two people who can be approached to provide a reference for you. One should be your last employer or someone from your last school or college, and the other can be someone who knows you well and can provide a character reference. The reference from your last employer can just be given as the Personnel Department of a large firm, if there is no particular person to write it for you. It is acceptable to put 'References available on request', but of course you have to ensure that they really are available immediately. I recommend that you give full details of two referees, to encourage potential employers to take your CV forward to the next stage of recruitment.

The reason for references is so that the reader can see that you have referees who are prepared to vouch for your competence and character. They will often be contacted, so you must make sure that you ask their permission first.

If you are sending your CV out to many addresses, make sure that your referees are happy about being contacted by a variety of people over a long period. You cannot afford to have an employer contact someone whose name you have given as a referee, only to be told that he or she does not want to vouch for you.

Character referees should normally have a good job of their own, and must not be in your own family, although if a family member has a different name from yours (such as an in-law), nobody would know that you were related. Family doctors or priests can often be prevailed upon to act as referees if they have known you for some time, but again you must get their permission first.

Include a telephone number for both references if possible, as the employer may well just decide to pick up the telephone on the spur of the moment. Before you give out home telephone numbers, check that this is acceptable to your referees. Always include e-mail addresses if you can, as many reference requests are sent out by e-mail. If you are applying for various vacancies it can be helpful to discuss the nature of each particular job with your referees to help them target the information they provide to the prospective employer.

Please remember that anyone who is prepared to write a reference for you is doing you a big favour. Regular appreciation makes sure all your referees feel properly valued by you.

If you have recently arrived in this country or have been travelling, and only have references from another country, I strongly advise you to contact the referees and get them to write an open letter or testimonial on your behalf. This can be used each time you send off your CV: send a photocopy (never send the original) of the letter, attached to the back of your CV.

The reason for this is that many employers are put off by the fact that it will take them a number of weeks to get a reference for you from abroad, but if they can see the testimonial in front of them, it may not prejudice them against you. In this case, only your two references are needed. Do not be tempted to include lots of photocopies of testimonials or exam certificates, as great wodges of paper will just put the employer off.

Typical problems

'I was sacked from my last job, and I know they will give me a bad reference.'

This can be overcome by using an earlier employer for the reference, and explaining why in an interview. You can say that you experienced personal difficulties in your last employment. You will have to rehearse your description of the events exactly, before any interview, to make sure that you can sound convincing. It may be worth spending some time reflecting on what went on in that job now that you have moved on. Looking back, what did you learn from the experience? Is there anything that you could have done differently? Most work relationships are affected by our own behaviour. Can you think of any positive points that you can bring from the last job to the next one?

If you have only had one job and been sacked, you will have to try and put the situation in the best light possible to explain what happened. Use two personal references on your CV. Perhaps you could do some voluntary work to give yourself another reference – even if only for a short time.

'I can get an excellent reference from my last employer, but she spends long periods out of the country. Should I still include her as one of my referees?'

Anything that is likely to put a prospective employer off is a bad idea. If the employer is interested in taking you on, he or she will not want to wait for six months before receiving your reference. I would advise you to find a substitute referee who can guarantee a quick response to any enquiries. Another alternative is to get an open testimonial from this woman explaining that she is often unavailable, which you could then include with your CV. You always need to work at making it as easy as possible for the employer to take your application further. It may well be worth substituting a glowing reference with a good one if it means that you get called for interview.

'I really can't put either of my last two employers as they know each other and I do not want my present boss to know I am applying for jobs. Is it all right for me just to put, "References available on request"'?

You can put this at the bottom of the CV. It means that you are stalling employers until they want to take your application further. While this may be totally reasonable, you also need to be aware that some employers may feel that you are making life harder for them than are other candidates who include full contact details for their referees right from the start.

How about putting one employer from longer ago? You could also put the last two employers down but ask that they not be contacted unless you are being invited to an interview.

Dos and don'ts

✔ Do get in an upbeat mood before you start work on this draft of your CV; it can make a big difference to your output.

✔ Do enhance your creative thinking by getting your environment as congenial as possible when you are working on the document.

✔ Do talk to people who have known you in different roles; they may come up with tasks, activities and achievements that you had forgotten.

✔ Do write normally, avoiding long words or phrases that you don't use in talking.

✔ Do avoid technical terms, abbreviations and jargon that won't be clear to all readers.

✗ Don't get bogged down in your own history. If the detail of one job escapes you, move on and think about another until your memory returns more clearly.

✗ Don't make things up. You need to be truthful about the work experience you have had. Even if what you write fools the employer, liars tend to get found out at the interview stage.

✗ Don't downplay your skills and experience by writing weak descriptions. Show off all the talents you have – every other candidate will do so too.

✗ Don't skimp on the information. Back your claims with examples and explanations.

✗ Don't lose your confidence halfway through. Stay enthusiastic in your tone.

Points to remember

1. Think widely about what you have done and include everything in your first draft.

2. You can always trim and edit your CV later but enlarging it may mean you have to start again from scratch.

3. Be positive when you describe your past activities; this can only impress any reader.

4. The first draft may not be perfect, but at least you have made a start.

5. If you leave some details out of your CV, keep the information in case you decide to include it in a later or different version.

Presentation

In this chapter we are going to look at the presentation of your CV. The way your CV looks is important and there are some major things to avoid. Understanding what puts the reader off can help us to present our CV in a more effective way.

Here are some of the most common errors made in presenting a CV.

The most common mistakes in CV presentation

- Having a messy layout with no clear structure.

- Putting too much material in each section, giving too much detail to read.

- Presenting events in an illogical sequence that is confusing.

- Writing in full sentences when bullet points would be more effective.

- Creating too fussy an appearance with different fonts, underlining and use of bold type all fighting with each other.

- Too much information overall, making the document too long.

▦ Using a poor-quality printer or scrappy paper for the CV.

After your work on collating material for the content of your CV, you are ready to consider how to present the document. The decisions you make about layout and presentation are as significant as the content you include.

You can now collect together all the material that you need to put into your CV. The way that you present the CV is of the utmost importance. You know that when you buy goods, you are often attracted by the packaging on the outside as much as by what is inside. The same is true of the CV. Giving employers your preparatory notes to read would leave them scratching their heads in confusion about what it all means, and they would probably not be very impressed.

After all, that is the whole point of compiling a CV in the first place. You want to present yourself in the best possible light to employers, and the way that they will judge you is by the impression they gain from those two sheets of A4 paper. That is the only information they have to go on. Everything in this chapter is to further the aim of them being really impressed by what they see.

When thinking about presenting your CV in the best way, try to avoid anything that might put an employer off. This means that the CV must look:

▦ Plain. An unadorned document says that you are businesslike and purposeful. Too many decorations, font variations and design complexities detract from an overall positive impression.

▦ Attractive. Choose a sans serif font or typeface for your document for an unfussy, compact style. Good fonts to use include Arial or Helvetica.

▦ Easy to read. Without wasting paper unnecessarily, you should allow generous margins and reasonable space between columns. Allow a clear line space after each paragraph to get more white space around your typing. Don't make your font size smaller than 11 as it will be too difficult to read.

Handwritten or typed?

Handwritten CVs are rarely seen, so you need to get your CV in typed form.

Get your CV done on a computer, even if you have to pay for the privilege. It will come out typed, can be edited without difficulty, and has the great advantage of being easily updated at any time in the future.

Do not attempt to produce your own document if you have never used a computer before and cannot type. It will take you ages and you will probably make many mistakes as well. You can pay to have your CV typed by somebody else, but shop around before you pay out a lot of money, to make sure that you get the best deal possible.

These days, many people have computers at home, and you may be able to find a friend or family member who will help you to get it done. The great advantages of computers are that you can make any corrections easily, you can produce different versions of your document and you can run off as many copies as you like, whenever you want them.

Ordering your material

While the information contained in most CVs is broadly the same, there are different ways of laying out your CV. Each style has its fans and users. The main difference lies in whether or not you have a personal profile, or description of what you have to offer, at the front of the CV or if it comes later on.

Traditional style

The order of the different sections recommended in the last chapter is traditional and has been tried and tested many times. The simplicity of the design seems to impress and interest employers.

The beauty of this standard layout is that the contents follow a logical pattern. First you are introducing yourself, then saying where you have come from, in terms of your education and employment experience. You then go on to explain your other skills, interests and any other relevant information, including what kind of person you are. Next comes an outline of what you can offer in the job, followed by details of your referees. You are telling the complete story.

Personal profile

An alternative way to order your material on the page is to have the additional information about your personality and achievements (sometimes called a 'personal profile') at the start of the document. This arrangement of contents means that the first thing that the reader sees is the paragraph explaining the special features about you. This is a more obviously direct and punchy way to start the CV and tends to be the dominant style in US CVs (or résumés), and it is now becoming increasingly common elsewhere. It allows readers to decide up front if they like the sound of the candidate or not. The advantage of having a personal profile at the beginning means that you can summarize early the contribution you can make, and hope to catch the eye of the selector in this way.

The slight drawback of this more forthright style is that readers may decide not to continue reading if they don't like what they see. In a pile of CVs, all with a positive, upbeat and vocal introduction, the reader can end up feeling jaded and may not read further than the first paragraph if it does not seem to be offering what is wanted. With the personal profile at the end of the CV, the reader is drawn or led through the whole document, and the personality of the writer is revealed only at the end. Examples of this style are shown on pages 104–06.

Other styles

CVs can be written in any style you like, with the information displayed in a variety of different layouts. That is the beauty of the document – you can select the order of the material that you feel will best reflect the contribution you can make to the job in question. If you feel that the employer will be more interested in a description of your relevant skills, you could choose to have these as subheadings through the document and then just summarize your educational and employment history elsewhere. See the example on pages 107–115 to illustrate this kind of tailored layout of a CV. If you feel that your work experience needs enlivening, you could add a separate subheading for 'Achievements' either under each position held or after the details of your jobs.

People choose different layouts for different reasons. If you left school with little or no qualifications, you may not want to have a large area for your education with not much to show. You could put your work experience first, followed later by your education and training all in a section together, which concentrates more on in-work training rather than schooldays.

What you must remember, though, is that the further you move away from the traditional model, the more your CV may look different from the others in the pile. For a vacancy in a more creative and fast-moving sector such as the arts or marketing, a more individual approach may be appreciated for its freshness and innovation. In the financial or legal sectors, it will probably be considered just flippant and peculiar and will be discarded.

Length

Your CV should not take up more than two or three sheets of A4 paper using one side only. Some people have difficulty in stretching their CVs past one side, particularly if they have little experience of work. Often a CV will stretch over four or five sides of A4 at the first draft. Let us look at each of these problems in turn.

Typical problems

'My CV is too short.'

If you have just left school it will be necessary to make your CV more of a personal information sheet. This gives you much more scope for including information about other activities that you have taken part in at school or college. For instance, you can describe your role in teams in which you have played or groups that you joined. See the example on pages 65–66 of Chapter 5.

If you took GCSEs at school you should be able to include your record of achievement, which charts your progress through years 10 and 11. You may wish to have one sheet of personal information with your record of achievement attached, or you could use the record to give you more details for your CV.

If you feel your CV just does not have enough in it to do your experience justice, you need to look at what you are including. You are probably doing too much unconscious self-editing as you go along. Stop yourself from making decisions too early about what to include. At this stage don't leave things out.

Put in everything – each job you have done, every training or college course and all your interests and skills. Have you done the exercise on pages 39–40 to describe your strong points? Most people find this tricky and resist compiling a list for themselves. In order to make your CV as full and as fascinating as it can be, you need to include some information about the sort of person you are.

Without working on the list, you won't be able to come up with much for the 'additional information' section, also known as the personal profile. This is the part of the CV that can really work for you in terms of securing your passage to the job interview, so bite the bullet, put aside your entirely natural feelings of modesty and embarrassment and fill in the list. Then create the paragraph from your 10 points that will make your CV fuller and longer. Don't let this omission scupper your chances of success.

'My CV is too long.'

You must reduce the length of your CV to two or three sides. Nobody ever reads more than three sides. Imagine you are a busy human resources officer desperately trying to check through the pile of CVs on your desk. With 20 to read in half an hour, you would find any excuse to reduce the pile by one.

The exceptions to this rule are older graduates who may have many college courses and jobs to fit in or those who have had many different jobs over a long time period. On no account should *any* CV be longer than three sides of A4 paper.

Even if you are an artist, actor or writer with a large body of work to your name, resist the temptation to list everything over many pages. If you must include a long list, then write the CV and follow it with an appendix of relevant work, performances or publications.

But if you are only just starting to get your CV in order, you have done well to create a first draft that is long enough for you to prune and edit properly now. Take each section in turn to see what you can shorten and reduce. Is one part much longer than another when you look at the whole document? Quite often, the employment section is longest and it is here that you can edit most profitably.

Use bullet points instead of full sentences and make sure that you are not duplicating any information. You may have done similar work in more than one position, but on the CV you only need to mention it once to get the credit for it. So if you were serving customers in every shop job you have had, try to vary the way you express it: 'solving clothing problems for customers', 'dealing with cash and credit card payments for goods', 'working as part of a team on the sales floor' are all different ways of stressing different skills used in retail.

Really work at cutting out all the material that does not add anything extra to your CV. Keep just the bare bones: saying less can often create more of an impact.

'My CV covers more than one side of A4, but only reaches halfway down the second.'

Stretch the whole document out (easy on a computer) until it covers the two sides easily. In other words, add more space around your name, to help it stand out, and make bigger gaps between the different sections. Place the referees one beneath the other instead of next to each other. The more white space showing on the CV, the easier it will be to read.

Read the answer to the first problem above too. It may be that you are just leaving your CV without enough information in it.

'I now have six pages of rough draft for my CV. How will it all fit on to two sides of A4?'

Be ruthless! Remember – keep it simple, make it clear, keep it short. Use brief phrases, in note form, for the details of your education and employment experience. If in doubt, throw it out! Edit your work to the bone, even if that means drafting the CV four or five times more. Make it look crisp and concise in the final version.

Layout

Dense, tightly packed typing is very difficult to read. Therefore spread out your words evenly and neatly on the page to aid the reader.

Use white or very light paper as it will often be photocopied once at the employer's premises and dark colours do not copy well. However, a heavier weight of paper is worth using as it can make your CV stand out from the rest. Buy a box of 100 gram weight paper, perhaps with friends to share the cost. Be careful to check though that the paper you buy will run through the printer you use. Some heavier paper creases and jams in certain more sensitive or older printers.

Keep it simple

I have seen a badly laid out CV in which the author had experimented with many different fonts or types of print. The result was a complete visual mishmash of styles and shapes. It put off anyone reading such a confusing document.

Never use more than two different fonts on your CV. More does not mean better-looking. Use different sizes of the same typeface if you want to add some definition for side headings but do not let them dominate the eye at the expense of the important details about you: your name, qualifications and job titles.

Adding emphasis

There are certain features about your CV that you will want to jump out at the reader. The main one is your name. If the employer is sifting through a pile of 20 CVs, you must make sure that yours is easy to spot and remember. Put your name in bold or in a slightly larger size font.

Other things to be put in bold, underlined or in some way highlighted are the level of exams you have taken (GCSEs, A levels, etc) and the position of each job that you have held (kitchen porter, journalist, marketing manager, etc). Do not be tempted to highlight the fact that the title of this document is Curriculum Vitae. If the reader cannot tell what the document is, he or she will not be giving it enough attention to act on it anyway. You also do not need to highlight the subheadings such as 'Personal details', etc through to 'References' either. Your details are what we want to call attention to, and the way to do that is to highlight your achievements in terms of your exams, or courses studied and your job titles.

Look at the examples of CVs in the next chapter to see how impressive this suggested layout looks.

A more creative or varied layout of your CV may possibly be appropriate if you work in a very design-conscious field, but generally I would advise caution. It is better to have a plainer document that is easy to read than a jazzy one that might put people off if they do not share your taste in graphics.

Sending your CV by e-mail

Rather than printing off your CV and posting it in application for a vacancy, you may want to use e-mail to send it to the employer. This could be because:

▓ You are sending the CV to an employer's or recruitment agency's website.

▓ You are circulating your CV to a range of employers on a speculative basis via the internet.

▓ The employer has specified in an advertisement that you should e-mail the CV.

▓ You are choosing e-mail because it suits your own administration better.

▓ You need to get the document there instantly.

Unless you have been specifically asked to e-mail the CV, if you are applying for a specific vacancy it is worth also sending a printed-out version on paper (also known as a 'hard copy') in the post afterwards. This is the form of the document that is preferred for photocopying and distributing by most employers and saves them the trouble of printing off the document themselves. It also ensures that you have sent a good-looking copy for them to see. Your beautiful e-mailed version may print out sadly askew on a different brand, style or age of printer.

If you are to e-mail the document it is even more important that you use simple fonts or typeface when putting it together on your computer. Arial and Helvetica are modern-looking, simply styled fonts that you can be more confident will print out properly at the employer's end. Make sure you write and save your CV in the Microsoft Word word-processing package as it otherwise may emerge with disturbed layouts or even as total gobbledygook if the employer's computer facilities do not match your own. Pages of incomprehensible rubbish spewing from the printer will not enhance the impression you are making!

Dos and don'ts

✔ Do show your CV to different people and ask for their opinion of the layout.

✔ Do check spelling and grammar if you are in any doubt about anything.

✔ Do spread the content evenly through the available space; it is kinder on the eye and encourages the reader to continue.

✔ Do save a plain-text version for future use.

✔ Do make a written note of which CV you send where.

✗ Don't leave anything in that you don't think adds to the total effect.

✗ Don't worry if the laying out of the CV is a fiddly business. It normally takes as long to get right as finding the content did.

✗ Don't photocopy your CV. If possible, print off fresh copies each time.

✗ Don't let your CV get out of date once it is done – keep refreshing it.

✗ Don't send out copies with mistakes in them. Spend time getting it to look as good as possible.

Points to remember

1. The look of your CV is at least as significant as what is in it.

2. You are in charge of choosing the best way of presenting the document.

3. A simple, uncluttered style says that you are a focused and professional applicant.

4. Unless you send a hard copy in the post, you cannot be sure how your e-mailed CV will look to the employer.

5. Use different sizes and styles of the same font rather than a mixture of different typefaces.

Guidelines and examples

Dos and don'ts

From the information that has been covered so far, we have seen that there are some general, basic rules to follow when making a good CV for yourself.

✔ Do keep it simple – avoid putting the reader off with long words or sentences.

✔ Do make it clear – all the information should be easy to understand.

✔ Do keep it short – two or three pages maximum. If in doubt about some material, throw it out.

✔ Do be positive – do not elaborate on jobs that you did not make a great success of, or finish; accent instead what you *did* achieve in the situation. For instance, even if you did not gain any exam passes at school or college, still list the subjects that you studied.

✔ Do remember that readers do not know what you did in your different jobs; the thing that you think is obvious may not be so to them.

✔ Do take time to put your CV together, and be prepared to make lots of rough notes about your career history first. Chapter 6 takes you through a step-by-step guide to getting started.

✔ Do experiment to see the effect of different aspects of your skills and achievements being highlighted.

✔ Do have two (or more) different versions of your CV if you need to apply for jobs in different career areas – but make sure to note which version of your CV you send off to each employer.

✔ Do get to know your CV inside out – to enable you to talk positively about yourself in an interview.

✔ Do update your CV whenever you have new experiences, qualifications or additional information to include.

✗ Don't use jargon, or you risk confusing and losing the reader.

✗ Don't use pretentious language; write as you would speak – simply and clearly.

✗ Don't copy someone else's CV – it will always look fake.

✗ Don't invent information – you may well have to prove your knowledge in an interview.

✗ Don't worry about boasting about your strengths – everybody else will be making themselves look extra good too.

> ✗ Don't run out of copies to send out – that will be the time when the job you *really* want comes up. Print out lots so that you always have a copy to hand.

Examples of CVs

The following pages contain 15 examples of CVs for people in different situations. One or more of them may be relevant to you, as you start to think about what to put in your own CV.

These examples are only included to give you an idea of the many different ways that CVs can be written. Although the names and addresses are fictitious, all the details have been taken from real examples of CVs that have helped people to get the jobs they want. See if you can identify how they use the points made earlier in this book about content and style.

There is not a CV for every situation, but the examples have been specially picked to represent a wide range of types of CV. Do not copy the information included in the examples, but see if any of them would be an appropriate model for you on which to base your own information.

These are the CVs that are included:

1. School leaver (Version 1)

2. School leaver (Version 2)

3. College leaver

4. Graduate (Version 1)

5. Graduate (Version 2)

6. Voluntary experience

7. Many jobs

8. Gaps between jobs

9. Woman returner
10. Career changer
11. After redundancy
12. Personal profile
13. Hybrid (Version 1)
14. Hybrid (Version 2)
15. Hybrid (Version 3).

1. School leaver (Version 1)

CV

Moira MAGUIRE
18 Horton Gardens
Nunhead Road
London
SE16 1QJ

Tel: 020 7338 0000
E-mail: mm@example.com*

EDUCATION:
Sept 2004–July 2009
Stone School, London SE16

Subjects studied:
English, mathematics,
science, history, drama

GCSEs:

English	C
Mathematics	C
Science	D

EMPLOYMENT:

June 2007 to date	Azir's Newsagent London SE16	**Newspaper deliverer:** Sorting out and delivering papers, dealing with the public and handling cash

WORK EXPERIENCE:
Since my final year at school I have worked with the elderly housebound. I regularly visit three people who live locally and help them with shopping and other household tasks. I find this work stimulating and rewarding, and intend to continue with it in my spare time.

OTHER SKILLS:
I was the House Captain in my last year at school and helped to organize assemblies and sports days. I have excellent keyboard skills and am confident at using a computer. I plan to learn to drive next year.

INTERESTS:**
Martial arts, bronze medal for swimming, competitive skateboarding, cookery and embroidery.

ADDITIONAL INFORMATION:
I am a polite and co-operative person and I apply myself totally to the task in hand. I am a member of my local youth group and regularly attend the swimming club. Since the third year I have been in the school drama group and have appeared in many productions.

REFERENCES:
Mr Azir (Proprietor)
Azir's Newsagent
218 Watermill Road
London
SE16 1HC

Tel: 020 7990 0000
E-mail: azira@example.com

Ms Hardcastle, Head Teacher
Stone School
Lovelace Road
London
SE16 3PP

Tel: 020 7731 0000
E-mail: headteacher@example.com

---

* Moira includes her e-mail address so that she can be contacted easily.
** Include a range of different interests to show all aspects of your personality.

Moira has had no full-time work yet, but has managed to get herself a part-time job delivering newspapers. This now provides evidence that she is capable of sticking to a work routine, is trustworthy and determined.

Even without this, she can write about her voluntary work experience working with old people while still at school. This implies that she has the ability to get on with a variety of different people, and shows her patience and her concern for others.

Her CV looks very different from most of the others on the following pages because she does not have a list of different jobs that she has done. However, although she has less information than many others, the fact that she has prepared a CV for herself will impress potential employers by setting her apart from other young people of her age.

She has included some interests which make her stand out from other school leavers – martial arts and skateboarding – which also give her topics to discuss at an interview.

Her CV is not much more than her personal details – in fact it could be called a 'Personal Information Sheet' rather than a CV – but it still tells the story of her career to date.

If you know that your own CV falls short in some area, eg little work experience or not many examination passes from school, then you need to find a way of compensating for this. You will need to show more evidence in different areas that make up for the gap. Moira does this by showing alternative work experience (part-time and voluntary) to make up for the fact that she has only just left school. Missing out on some area of experience or qualifications need not be an insurmountable hurdle to impressing an employer. You just need to show that what you lack in one area you more than make up for in another.

2. School leaver (Version 2)

CV

Alex SAMUELS
77 High Slopes
Penarth
Cardiff
CF2 1LL

Tel: 02252 000000
Mobile: 07700 000000
E-mail: alsam@example.com

EDUCATION:
2000–2005
Forest Boys School, Penarth CF3

GCSEs:

English Literature	C
English Language	C
Mathematics	C
ICT	C
Religious Studies	C

2005–2007
Bluebank Sixth Form College, Penarth CF3

A Level course:
Business Studies – finance, management
Psychology – case studies
Media Studies – camera shots, studying films
ICT – spreadsheets, databases

EMPLOYMENT:

2004	Credit Suisse Canary Wharf London E3	**Work experience in ICT department** Creating computer system to view and fix any problems or errors. Doing internet research.
2007	Flower Shop Penarth CF3	**Sales assistant** Wrapping flowers, advising customers, refilling pots, taking payment, responsible for shop in absence of manager.
2008	Building company Penarth CF3	**Builder's labourer** Digging, mixing cement, shifting building materials, taking measurements.
2008	Courier company Penarth CF3	**Driver's assistant** Organizing removals, transporting people's furniture and belongings from one place to another, packing boxes and loading vans.

OTHER SKILLS:
I can speak basic Spanish (my father's family come from Spain) and am taking up Spanish lessons so I can improve my speaking ability in that language. I also have good ICT skills and can easily find my way around a computer without any problems. I have used various different programs including Excel, PowerPoint, Photoshop and Internet Explorer and often find myself helping family and friends when they get stuck.

INTERESTS:
I have many interests in life, the main one being sport. I enjoy watching and playing most sport especially when Wales are competing, eg rugby and football. I also regularly play football at the weekend with a local team and represented my school at football when I was a pupil. Playing football is important to me because it is a team game and it has taught me to work and

communicate effectively with other people. As well as playing football to keep fit, I regularly go running in the evenings and get enjoyment from a good workout in the gym.

Another interest of mine is music. I often go to see live music and groups in concerts and enjoy listening to a wide range of music, from the Kings of Leon to 50 Cent. I find music a good way to relax and like listening to different types depending what mood I am in.

ADDITIONAL INFORMATION:
I am a hard-working person who always puts 100 per cent effort into any task I am faced with. Careful work is important to me, so each job I am involved in is done to the best of my ability. I am reliable and have good timekeeping skills and finish any work set within the deadline. I am a fast learner and am quick to pick up new ideas and team skills. I am an outgoing and sociable person who gets on easily with people and works very well with others and in groups. However, I am just as capable of working independently and motivating myself. I have a lot to offer and am keen and full of energy.

REFERENCES:
Sylvia Jones
Florist
1 Main Street
Penarth
Cardiff
CF2 5RG

Tel: 08994 00000
E-mail: sylvia@example.com

Rachel Stevens
Author
64 Tudor Gardens
London
W31 5RD

Tel: 020 7554 0000
E-mail: rs@example.com

Alex did not have the best time at school. A series of difficulties at home meant that he did not do as well as expected at his GCSEs. His subsequent experience at college was not much better as he was not in a position to benefit from studying at that time and he left without taking any A-level exams. He puts his A-level subjects down on his CV, however, as he wants to get the credit for the studying he has done even though it did not result in exam passes.

After a variety of jobs he is hoping to progress to something with better prospects than the small businesses for which he has worked so far. He stresses the variety of experience that he has and the level of responsibility that he has been given. He wants to create the impression of a bright, reliable and trustworthy employee.

Alex was disappointed by his college experience and now is very keen to move on and get ahead. His description of himself on the narrative parts of the CV shows that he is a lively and engaging young man. He wants employers to think that he is someone who would be an asset to a team and would prove to have a lot of potential if he were given a chance to show what he could do.

Rewriting

Alex came to me for help as he had never written a CV before and he was worried that he did not have much to be proud of. He found it very hard to boast about himself and did not really know where to start. He began by talking to me about the interests that he had and wrote a list of his 10 best character strengths. It was the first time that he had made such a list about himself. His list read: hard-working; reliable; good timekeeper; sociable; good team player; motivated; sensible; likeable; bright; learns quickly. You will see how he turned this list into 'Additional Information' in the first version below.

The CV above was the third version that he wrote. As well as adding information to the main tasks of each of his jobs throughout the redrafting process, Alex made most alterations to the second page of his CV. Take a look at the three versions side by side to see how he began, improved it and then reached the final version. These show how the editing and reshaping process worked for him.

Version 1 – Alex's first draft

Interests:
I have many interests in life the main one being sports. I enjoy watching and playing most sport especially football. I also play football at the weekend with my mates and was in my school football team. I go running in the evenings and get enjoyment from a good workout in the gym.

Another interest of mine is music. I see live music and go to gigs and enjoy listening to a wide range of music from kings of Leon to 50 Cent.

Other Skills:
I can speak basic Spanish and am taking up Spanish lessons so I can improve. I also have good ICT skills and can easily find my way around a computer without any problems.

Additional Information:
I am a hardworking person who always puts a 100% effort into any task I am faced with. I am reliable and have good time keeping skills and finish any work set within the deadline. I'm an outgoing and sociable person who gets on really well with people and works very well with others and in groups however I can work independently too.

Version 2 – Alex's second draft
After discussing it with me and working on his CV a little more, here is his second version. Alex's fairly dismal experience at college was never going to be the most impressive thing about his background, so I suggested he add more material to describe

more about himself and to speak up more about his strengths, as this was the main way he could make an impact on an employer.

Interests:
I have many interests in life the main one being sports. I enjoy watching and playing most sport especially when Wales are participating like rugby and football. I also regularly play football at the weekend with my mates and have represented my school football team during my time there. As well as playing football to keep fit I regularly go running in the evenings and get enjoyment from a good workout in the gym.

Another interest of mine is music. I regularly go to see live music gigs and enjoy listening to a wide range of music from kings of Leon to 50 Cent.

Other Skills:
I can speak basic Spanish and am taking up Spanish lessons so I can improve. I also have good ICT skills and can easily find my way around a computer without any problems.

Additional Information:
I am a hardworking person who always puts a 100% effort into any task I am faced with. I am reliable and have good time keeping skills and finish any work set within the deadline while keeping the work at a high level of quality. I'm an outgoing and sociable person who gets on really well with people and works very well with others and in groups however I am just as capable of working independently and motivating myself.

Version 3

In the final version, the one featured in this section, Alex tidied up the CV and sorted out its presentation. He broke up the writing slightly and put capital letters in the right places. He altered the language so that it contained less slang – eg substituting 'concerts' for 'gigs' – and constructed more even paragraphs so that it looked easy to read.

He has a nice writing style that still shines out through all the alterations. It was important that the CV still read like the self-penned CV of a 19-year-old young man but without putting off the older, more traditional reader.

3. College leaver

CV

Robin FOSTER
222 Upper Street
London
N1 5DJ

Tel: 020 7278 0000
E-mail: rfoster@example.com

EDUCATION:

1999– 2004	Kingsmere Secondary School London E5	**GCSEs:** English C, Maths B, Physics B, Chemistry C, Geography B, Biology B, Sociology B, French E
2004– 2006	South West London College London SW15	**A levels:** Maths A, Biology C Physics E
2006– 2009	Peele University Peele Northants	**BA Social Science:** Studied economics, history, politics, philosophy, geography and statistics* **Specialized in:** Development studies. My thesis was on Third World debt

EMPLOYMENT:

Both my jobs have been part time, and took place during vacations and evenings while at college.

| 2007 | Peele University Union | **Bar Attendant**
Serving customers,
handling cash,
cleaning and stocking
bar area. |
| 2008 | Peele University Catering | **Catering Assistant**
Preparing food,
serving at events,
dealing with guests,
cleaning kitchens. |

OTHER SKILLS:

I am familiar with PowerPoint and Excel packages.**

INTERESTS:

Keep-fit (I was a member of several sports societies while at college), reading, travel, music.

ADDITIONAL INFORMATION:

Having successfully completed my course at Peele University, I am looking to gain employment in an administrative capacity, general office work, or work involving figures. I always contribute fully and would enjoy maintaining high standards of accuracy and attention to detail. I am keen to start my career and would be a loyal and dependable employee.

REFERENCES:

Professor S Welt	Dr L M Cash
Peele University	97 The Crescent
Peele	London
Northants	W5 2PB
NT5 5BG	
Tel: 01772 00000	Tel: 020 8435 0000
E-mail: swelt@example.ac.uk	E-mail: lmc@example.com

> * Give full details of the courses you studied if you have only recently left college.
> ** Explain which computer packages you can use.

Robin has made the most of the space available to him to give full information about his college career. He has given detailed information about his course at college and about the jobs he did while studying. Without any full-time work experience, he needs to bring out any other factors which may help to persuade a future employer that he is worth taking on.

He mentions his active involvement in sport to show that he has a variety of interests. He also uses the 'Additional Information' section as a chance to sell himself to the employer. He stresses his good points to show the contribution he could make.

He knows that he has to use his CV to enable the employer to envisage him at work. His main selling point is the potential contribution he could make if employed. Robin makes clear in the 'Additional Information' section that administrative work and figure work are areas where he thinks he could make the strongest application. He could well be sending this CV off on a speculative basis in case vacancies arise at a specific company or organization.

4. Graduate (Version 1)

CV

Michael SMITH*
935 Main Road
Manchester
M16 8AP

Tel: 0161 693 0000
E-mail: msmith@example.com

Education:

1995–2002	Frankwell Secondary School Shrewsbury Shropshire	**GCSEs:** Seven subjects including English Language, Literature and Mathematics
		A levels: Mathematics B, Geography C
2002–2005	Lowston University Lowston Surrey	**BA (Hons) Business Studies:** Specialized in marketing and financial management
2007–2008	London Massage School London SW18	**ITEC Course in Massage, Anatomy and Physiology:** Training in techniques to give professional, therapeutic treatment, allied with a sound knowledge of the systems of the body and their relevance to massage
2008 to date	London Massage School London SW18	**Intermediate Massage Training Course:** Continued training by studying shiatsu, medical massage, reflexology and breathing and relaxation techniques

Employment:

2007 to date	Private work in the London area	**Consultant Masseur:** Relaxing, professional therapeutic massage with essential oils
2005– 2007	Employment agencies in the London area	**Various clerical positions:** General office work and dealing with the public

Other skills:
I have a working knowledge of aromatherapy, reflexology and shiatsu. I have a current, clean driving licence and have recently acquired basic keyboard skills.

Additional information:
I have always used my hands in a creative way, and found massage a natural progression, which is immensely rewarding and fulfilling.

I am a friendly, outgoing person, and am able to get on with people in all situations. I am reliable, trustworthy, punctual and meticulous. I have the ability to work well as part of a team, can deal competently with administrative duties and particularly enjoyed the financial aspects of my business course.

Referees:

Bernadette Beckett (Principal)	Clare Maledy (Course Tutor)
London Massage School	BA Business Studies
Westcliffe Road	Lowston University
London	Lee Street
SW18 2HB	Lowston
	Surrey
	KT3 2MN
Tel: 020 8339 0000	Tel: 020 8448 0000
E-mail: BB@example.ac.uk**	E-mail: clarem@example.ac.uk

> *   Put your family name or surname in capital letters.
> ** Include referees' e-mail addresses for ease of contact.

Michael is trying to use his massage qualification to get a job in a health or sports centre. However, his background is in business studies, so he uses the 'Additional information' section of his CV to explain his interest in massage.

He gives most details about his interest in massage, the subjects that he studied in his practical training and the fact that he has spent a period successfully self-employed as a masseur.

He is still considering a career in business, so he has created another CV, to apply for a different type of work, and which you can see on the next page.

Sometimes you can have more than one career in mind. You may have talents that lie in different directions or just want to keep your options open. If you are just starting your working life, you may not yet have decided what will suit you best in the long term. You may have recently retrained, as Michael has, and be trying to diversify. In this case you may well need more than one CV to reflect adequately your different career possibilities. With two documents you can stress separate aspects of your skills and abilities to tailor your CV for the particular career in question.

5. Graduate (Version 2)

CV

Michael SMITH
935 Main Road
Manchester
M16 8AP

Tel: 0161 693 0000
Mobile: 07813 00000*
E-mail: msmith@example.com

EDUCATION:

1995–2002	Frankwell Secondary School Shrewsbury Shropshire	**GCSEs:** Seven subjects including English Language, Literature and Mathematics
		A levels: Mathematics B, Geography C
2002–2005	Lowston University Lowston Surrey	**BA (Hons) Business Studies:** Specialized in marketing and financial management, completed thesis on European business training
2007–2008	London Massage School London SW18	**ITEC Course in Massage, Anatomy and Physiology:** Training in techniques to give all types of massage, currently studying at intermediate level

EMPLOYMENT:

| 2007 to date | Self-employed in the London area | **Consultant Masseur:** Relaxing, professional therapeutic massage with essential oils |
| 2005– 2007 | Employment agencies in the London area | **Various clerical positions:** Dealing with the public and filing, answering phone calls, writing letters, typing, keeping petty cash account |

OTHER SKILLS:
I am a keen masseur, and have a working knowledge of aromatherapy, reflexology and shiatsu. I have a current, clean driving licence and have recently acquired keyboard skills.

ADDITIONAL INFORMATION:
I enjoyed my degree course which introduced me to the business world. I specialized in financial analysis and the marketing function, and completed my thesis on the different types of business trading across Europe.

I am a friendly, outgoing person, and am able to get on with people in all situations. I am reliable, trustworthy, punctual and meticulous. I have the ability to work well as part of a team, can deal competently with administrative duties and am keen to establish my career in a clerical or administrative capacity.**

REFEREES:

Clare Maledy (Course Tutor)	Bernadette Beckett (Principal)
BA Business Studies	London Massage School
Lowston University	Westcliffe Road
Lee Street	London
Lowston	SW18 2HB
Surrey	
KT3 2MN	
Tel: 020 8448 0000	Tel: 020 8339 0000
E-mail: Clarem@example.ac.uk	E-mail: BB@example.ac.uk

> * Include your mobile number if you think the employer may want to contact you quickly.
> ** Give clear indicators about how you can be useful to an employer.

It would be difficult for Michael to have just one CV which detailed all the information that he needs to apply for both the types of work that he is interested in. As these are really two distinct areas, he needs a CV for each.

His second CV has the same basic information about his personal details, qualifications and experience, but stresses his interest in a career in administration instead of massage. He includes more information about his college course, his office experience and changes the 'Additional information' section to appeal more to employers of clerical staff.

These two CVs, sent out with care to appropriate employers, will enhance his chances of gaining one of the types of employment of his choice.

This example shows that Michael has created two impressive documents to reflect his job hunting. If he had relied on just one CV, he would have found it difficult to straddle both options while making the CV interesting. By creating the second, more business-oriented CV he can keep the focus of each targeted at the kind of employers he would like to work for, highlight the respective skills and aptitudes he has and show the full contribution that he could make in each case.

6. Voluntary experience

CV

Geraldine CLARKE
99 Eugenia House
Norton Street
Chipping Campden
Gloucestershire
GL2 1KK

Tel: 016732 0000
E-mail: gc@example.com

Education

1994– 1999	Josiah Wedgwood School London NE21	**GCSEs:** English, Maths, French, Technical Drawing and Art
1999– 2003	North London Technical College London NE17	**BTEC National Diploma:** Visual research, objective drawing, furniture design, drawing office practice, foundation science, industrial organization
		BTEC Higher National Diploma: Antique history and restoration specializing in gilding and Victoriana

Voluntary experience

2003– 2009	Green World Bath Avon	**Membership Secretary:*** Dealing with all letter and phone enquiries, setting up new IT system and helping to train paid staff

Hobbies and interests

I enjoy photography, reading, windsurfing, sailing, skiing and going to the cinema and theatre.

Additional information

Since leaving college, I have been looking after a sick relative. I used my two free days each week to volunteer for a local charity. During the last six years I have become very involved in their business, and have recently been part of a team which designed and established a new computerized membership system.

Although this work is unpaid, the skills I have gained are those used in any business environment, such as being part of a team, keeping to deadlines, working under pressure and delegating tasks.

I enjoyed learning all about providing efficient services for our members and see this area of work as very similar to customer care in the commercial sector.** It is important to be able to analyse and anticipate the needs of members, communicate clearly with them and follow up all enquiries quickly and effectively.

I am now keen to start applying these skills in an organization, where I can make a full contribution to high standards of customer service.

References

Mr J Phillips	Mr M Baldock (Director)
BTEC Graphic Design	Green World, Hunerk House
Course Director	99 North Street
North London Technical College	Bath
Swift Road	Avon
London	BR4 2JK
NE178 3PU	
Tel: 020 8830 0000	Tel: 01382 00000
E-mail: phillipsj@example.com	E-mail: baldock@example.com

> * Put all job titles in bold type.
> ** Explain how your skills are transferable to the work you want to do.

Geraldine has only ever done voluntary work, but she uses the 'Additional information' section to explain why. She had sensibly chosen voluntary work in the field in which she wanted to work, so is able to stress what useful experience she has gained.

Her years of volunteering have also gained her a glowing reference from the director of the charity concerned.

It is important for Geraldine that she makes as much of her voluntary experience as any other candidate would from paid work. She pulls out the main tasks that she contributed, evaluates the new areas that she has learnt about and describes those aspects that she particularly enjoyed. Employers are always interested in the motivation of applicants. It enables them to see if the things that inspired you in your previous work are linked to the work being offered in the current vacancy. An enthusiastic candidate will shine even at the stage of submitting CVs or paper applications.

You can use your CV to confront any prejudices that employers may have about you. At first glance, Geraldine's work history is not very impressive. After studying arts subjects, she has not even had one 'proper' job. Employers may be tempted to assume that she is:

■ lazy;

■ unable to hold down a job;

■ undisciplined;

■ not a team player;

■ stuck in a rut;

■ not interested in learning;

■ not ambitious.

In fact Geraldine is none of these things. She had to relinquish her career plans to look after her younger sister who was badly injured in a car crash. She explicitly confronts each of these possible perceptions by providing evidence of the contrary:

■ Her hobbies show her active outlook.

■ Her volunteering experience is evidence of her employability.

■ Her six years of voluntary work show her rigour and discipline.

■ She gives evidence of working as part of a team.

■ She offers insight into best commercial practice and illustrates how she enjoys learning.

■ She finishes by stating that she sees herself at the start of a new phase of career development.

The overall effect is that the employers would consider themselves lucky to get such a talented applicant – even though she has not had one paid job before. This, of course, is just the impression Geraldine was aiming for.

7. Many jobs

CV*

Adam PETERS
3 Upland Street
London
SE21 1ST

Tel: 020 8946 0000

EDUCATION:

Sept 1993– May 1997	Greens' School London SE3	**Subjects studied:** English, maths, science, art, metalwork, woodwork
Sept 1998– July 2000	Central College London SW1	**Which Job? Course**

EMPLOYMENT:

Aug 2006– Mar 2009	Freshfood Dairies London SW16	**Milk roundsman:** Bookkeeping, dealing with the public, handling cash, ordering stock, banking and deliveries
Sept 2005– Apr 2006	True Personnel London E16 1HH	**Recruitment consultant:** Recruitment advertising, interviewing, wages, canvassing for new business, general office duties
July 2003– Aug 2005	Bales' Business Services London SE17 1JD	**Warehouseman:** Storing valuable data files, keeping accurate records, dealing with clients
Mar 1998– July 2003	Various temporary agencies around London, working as a general assistant and in manual work	

Aug 1996– Mar 1998	Jay's Stores London SE6 3RT	Cashier: Shelf-filling, responsible for cash, checking all deliveries, ordering shop stock

INTERESTS:

Squash, snooker, swimming, bowling, crosswords, collecting stamps, walking my dog.

ADDITIONAL INFORMATION:

I am always keen to take on extra responsibility at work. I am trustworthy and hard-working and have often worked overtime in my previous jobs.

My varied work experience has taught me a great deal about different types of organizations and I am confident at joining in quickly in any new position. I am a fast learner.

I would like to work in a position which involves contact with the public, as I get on well with a wide variety of people. I enjoy being part of a team, but can also work alone and unsupervized.

REFERENCES

Mr Hugh MacKinnon (Foreman at Bales' Business Services)** 14 Beach House Brighton Road London SE21 1HF	Mr Adrian Smithson (Accountant) 134 Eugenia Road London SW4 4TL
Tel: (work) 020 7493 0000 E-mail: HMac@example.com	Tel: (work) 020 8699 0000 E-mail: ads@example.com

---

* You can abbreviate 'Curriculum Vitae' to 'CV'.
** Include the job title of your referee to show his or her role in the organization.

Adam has plenty of jobs listed on his CV already. He has grouped together some of his work experience, between 1998 and 2003, to cut further jobs out. Those that he is omitting only duplicate the jobs that he has listed in full elsewhere.

He gives full details of some jobs to show the skills that he has learnt, grouping others together instead of listing them all.

Adam also has possible prejudices to overcome in the mind of potential employers. His rapid job changes over the years could worry anyone thinking of employing him in case it indicates a lack of persistence or determination. It could be the case that each of Adam's previous employers had been unhappy with his attitude or performance and that he had been encouraged to leave each job. Adam is keen to show that, although he may only have stayed for a short time in each place, he gave good value when he was there.

Many of us go through a period of trying out different types of work before we settle for one particular area. In fact the variety of practical work that Adam has been doing is quite consistent but just reflects the insecure nature of such work. More frequent job changing is becoming the norm in the modern world of work rather than the old pattern of spending years in one organization. Promotion is normally gained now through moving to a different employer as hierarchies get flatter and prospects are limited accordingly.

In Adam's case, he is indeed someone who gets restless after too long in one place but he maintains his enthusiasm for work by moving on and starting with a new employer doing roughly similar work. This CV details all the different abilities that he has acquired over the years, which vary from clerical work to practical skills. He knows that demonstrating this will be vital if he is to get a job interview from his CV. His varied experience needs to show up as relatively more advantageous than his rapid moves are disadvantageous.

8. Gaps between jobs

CV

Shola ODUNTAN
25b Aubert Road
Birmingham
B15 1NS

Tel: 0121 661 0000
E-mail: s.oduntan@example.com

NATIONALITY: Nigerian (with full British citizenship)

EDUCATION:

1993–1998*	Government College Lagos, Nigeria	**O levels:** 5 subjects including English
1998–2000	Bournebrook College Birmingham B29	**Course in Business Studies**

EMPLOYMENT:

2007–2009	Njoku Industries Birmingham B3	**Marketing Assistant:** Responsible for all the marketing support activity for the company, producing and administering direct mail campaigns, creating and maintaining databases, planning, designing and implementing advertising, organizing exhibitions, setting market budgets

---

2003–	Gold and Sons	**Advertisement Production**
2005	Birmingham B12	**Manager:** Organizing plans and advert layouts, liaising with clients and advertising agents, designers, printers, proof-reading and passing pages for filming and setting deadlines for the sections

ADDITIONAL INFORMATION:
In 2001 I travelled extensively in Africa with a relative, supporting myself through trading activities. In 2006 I toured Europe, doing temporary, seasonal work. These periods of travelling have given me the opportunity to learn a great deal about other countries and cultures, and I have seen many different ways of organizing businesses and society in general.

OTHER SKILLS:
During the last year, I have used a local resource centre to learn keyboarding and computer skills and am now able to use QuarkXpress, a desk-top publishing package. I can speak four different African languages and basic French.**

INTERESTS:
Reading, listening to music, gardening, yoga and aerobics, writing short stories. I recently entered a national competition with my work.

REFERENCES:

Mrs A Collins	Mr O Burkitt
Personnel Director	Director
Njoku Industries	Gold and Sons
Wyndham Industrial Estate	25 Field Lane
Mill Lane	Birmingham
Birmingham	B12 6LQ
B3 2DD	
Tel: 0121-572 0000	Tel: 0121-283 0000
E-mail: ac@example.com	E-mail: oburkitt@example.com

> * Just years will do – you don't need to include months or dates.
> ** Skills in different languages will always be appreciated.

In order to explain the fact that she has had long gaps in her career history, Shola gives details about the periods that she spent travelling. She stresses the benefits that these periods have given her and shows how she has developed as a person.

She has only had two jobs so far and so she makes sure that she lists all the key tasks that she undertook in each place. If, like Shola, you know that there is one aspect of your CV that will need explaining, make sure you offer the details that are required. Any reader of this CV would wonder at the gaps between college and her first job, and between her two posts. Shola has ensured that she not only explains what she was doing during these periods but that she sells them as giving her advantages and skills not available to other candidates. The fact that she speaks four African languages could be invaluable to a company trading across that continent.

9. Woman returner

CV

Barbara ANDERSON
9 Redlands Tower
Culvert Road
Sidcup
Kent
DA15 3TT

Mobile: 07813 00000*

EDUCATION:

1993–1998	Sacred Heart Grammar School Sidcup Kent	GCSEs: 5 subjects including English
1998–2000	Sidcup Technical College Sidcup Kent	A levels: English C, History C

EMPLOYMENT:

Sept 2000–June 2004	Department of Employment Unemployment Benefit Office Mottingham Kent	Executive Officer: Supervising staff, organizing work, dealing with the public, sorting out IT problems

OTHER SKILLS:
I am computer literate and have a good working knowledge of Word and Excel.**

INTERESTS:
I enjoy reading historical novels and biographies, going to the cinema and joining in outdoor activities with my children. I am part of a group of concerned friends and neighbours that looks after our local park.

ADDITIONAL INFORMATION:
I was a prefect at school. In June 2004, I left the Civil Service to bring up my two young children. As a full-time mother since that date, I have acquired new skills, such as the ability to organize and communicate on different levels, to use my imagination, and to be patient and flexible. I am a focused and motivated person with a loyal and determined attitude. I enjoy solving work problems, endeavour tirelessly for the sake of my team, and would love to use my skills to bring success to my next employer.

REFERENCES:
Ms Irene Hill
22 Stafford Road
High Wycombe
Buckinghamshire
HW1 1LD

Tel: 01291 00000
E-mail: ihill@example.com

Father Paul Behan
Parish Priest
Church of Our Lady
Crimscott Lane
London
WC2B 1YB

Tel: 020 7832 0000
E-mail: fatherb@example.com

---

* Just put your mobile number if you prefer to be contacted that way.
** Make the most of what skills you have, so that an employer will know that you don't need training in those areas.

Barbara is anxious to get back to work after bringing up her young children. She sensibly stresses the skills that she has acquired during her time in the home and emphasises how keen she is to re-establish her career.

She gives full details of her previous job and shows that she has many interests.

Many women are apologetic if they have been out of the labour market for a while. Describing their activity as 'only bringing up my children' or as 'just a housewife', they downplay the skills that they have been developing during this period. In fact, raising children is hard work and demands many abilities that are not always obvious to other people. Other assets that might apply to someone in Barbara's position include:

- tolerance;

- patience;

- determination;

- confidence;

- using own initiative;

- being a self-starter;

- solving disputes;

- good memory;

- quick thinking;

- setting boundaries and establishing discipline and routines;

- problem solving;

- project management;

- administration;

- managing finances;

- being an effective entertainer!

If you have been bringing up children, make the most of the skills you have to offer as a result. Be proud of this really important work in which you have been engaged and talk up what you have to offer an employer as a result.

10. Career changer

CV

Marilyn BROWNE
806 Tiverton Place
London   Tel: 020 8928 0000
N5 2HX*   E-mail: mbrowne@example.com

Education

1990– 1995	Ragdale School Birmingham B14	**0 levels:** English A, Biology B, Maths B, History C, Chemistry B
1995– 1997	Charing Court Hospital London W5	**Pupil Nurse for State** **Enrolled Nurse** Full training in a range of nursing skills

Employment

Nov 2004– Jan 2009	Queen's Hospital London SE3	**State Enrolled Nurse:** Working in theatre with the Sister, making sure theatre list is correctly written, that theatre is ready for use, instruments are correct for different operations, teaching student nurses, completing appropriate paperwork, liaising between hospital departments, taking phone calls
June 2000– Aug 2004	Waterside Hospital London W1	**State Enrolled Nurse:** Looking after medical and surgical patients, doing ward rounds with doctors, making sure that patients' notes were up to date, transferring patients to theatre, dealing with enquiries, dispensing drugs

Nov 1997– May 2007	Charing Court Hospital London W5	**State Enrolled Nurse:** Working in out-patients' department making sure patients' notes were completed, getting doctors' trays ready for examination, answering phone calls, dealing with patients and medical sales representatives

Interests

Horse riding, badminton, walking my dog, learning keyboard skills, reading nursing journals.

Additional information

My working life to date has been mainly caring for people. This has made me patient and tolerant when dealing with the public. In hospital, patients and their relatives are often extremely scared and distressed, even angry, and they need calm but firm handling.

As a result of my State Enrolled Nurse training, I am familiar with the study of biology, chemistry and drugs, and have had 13 years' experience as a qualified nurse working in a variety of different medical establishments.

I now wish to use my professional skills in combination with my main interest, which is caring for animals.** I feel my nursing skills together with my trustworthy, hard-working and dedicated character, would make me ideally suited to a career as an animal nurse.

References

Mr Simon Howarth (Theatre Manager)
Queen's Hospital
London
SE3 2HJ
Tel: 020 7339 0000
E-mail: simonh@example.com

Mrs J Michaels
21 Green Vale
London
SE16 2KY
Tel: 020 7231 0000
E-mail: jmichaels@ example.com

> * Always include your full postcode.
> ** Give your reasons for wanting a change of career and stress your transferable skills.

Marilyn wants to change her career after nearly 15 years studying and working in nursing. Although her experience will be highly appropriate for her desired career in animal nursing, she needs to justify her decision to change her plans after such a long period in one career.

By using the 'Additional information' section to explain her ideas, she can answer the questions which any future employer may have. This is important because an employer just flicking through a pile of CVs may not grasp that Marilyn wishes to change career direction unless she makes this fact stand out clearly in the document. Many people decide to take their skills and use them in a different way during their working lives. It may be that you find out about a new career after you have been working in one area for a while or you may just change your mind about what suits you best. You may find that you have changed as a person and need new and different challenges to motivate you.

If you are in this position, it is up to you to establish your credentials for the new direction you wish to take. This will mean showing what transferable skills you have that will be applicable to your desired new option. Marilyn spent some time establishing where the parallels lay between what she had been doing and what she wanted to change to. In her 'Additional Information' she includes three paragraphs that explain how her experience, skills and personality respectively are all suited to working as an animal nurse. This outline cannot help but impress the reader and will encourage her candidature to be taken seriously as a result.

11. After redundancy

CV

Melanie RANDALL
5 Somerfield Street
London
SW9 4LH

Tel: 020 7889 0000
E-mail: melanie@example.com

EDUCATION:

1994–1999	Trinity School London SE8	**GCSEs:** English, Mathematics, Art, Geography, Home Economics

EMPLOYMENT:

2007–2009	Popular Pizzas London EC2	**Senior Assistant:** In charge of seven staff, organizing work rotas, ordering stock, cashing up, recruitment and training of staff, dealing with sales representatives
2004–2007	Popular Pizzas London EC2	**Catering Assistant:** Helping to prepare fast food, general kitchen work, waiting at table and handling cash
2001–2003	Newgate Inn London E3	**Kitchen Supervisor:** In charge of busy kitchen, menu planning, cooking, cleaning, stock control, bookkeeping, banking and staff supervision*

| 1999–2001 | Newgate Inn London E3 | **Kitchen Assistant:** Helping out with serving, preparing food, and running special events |

INTERESTS:

Listening to music, reading, cooking and entertaining, and playing pool and darts. I arrange charity darts and pool matches for the Multiple Sclerosis Society.**

ADDITIONAL INFORMATION:

I am punctual, reliable and able to work enthusiastically under pressure, either within a team or alone. I am a straightforward, positive and a fair person with a friendly disposition and a good sense of humour. This has aided me in the supervision of staff and in extensive dealings with clients and the public.

I am always keen to contribute fully to every company I work for. I have been promoted in both my jobs and this reflected the high regard in which my skills were held.

I have been in positions of trust, handling money on behalf of others. I have a strong ethical outlook and am well-balanced and controlled. My aim is to find employment in an environment with high standards and productivity.

REFERENCES:

Dick Nye	Desmond Cook
Manager	Area Manager
The Newgate Inn	Popular Pizzas
Newgate Street	New Road
London	London
E3 3FG	EC2 3LR
Tel: 020 7447 0000	Tel: 020 7831 0000
E-mail: nye@example.com	E-mail: cookd@example.com

* Play up the responsibilities you had – if you were ever in charge, say so.
** If you take the lead in any of your hobbies, include the details here.

Melanie had the misfortune to be made redundant, not once but twice, from her jobs in the catering trade. The first time it happened she had to start in a more lowly post and work her way back up again to a more responsible position – and now she has to begin again.

It is more difficult to find employment once you are unemployed, so she has filled the 'Additional Information' section with as much positive information about herself as possible. The 'Interests' section shows the charity fund-raising work with which she is involved, all of which adds to the impression that she has a lot to offer.

Melanie knows that a whole range of stereotypes can face someone who is out of work. She found out the first time she was made redundant that it was a slow process to get another job. Some of the assumptions that could be made about her are that she is:

■ unemployable;

■ bound to be depressed;

■ unmotivated;

■ not able to keep to work routines or be disciplined;

■ bitter about her bad luck;

■ probably introverted;

■ someone with not much to offer;

■ an unreliable employee.

To combat these unfair and incorrect prejudices that she might face, she writes a positive and confident couple of paragraphs about her skills and personality in her 'Additional information' section. The overall effect is upbeat and noticeable.

12. Personal profile

CV
FOR STEPHEN DEERY

PERSONAL PROFILE:*
An analytical and proactive general manager with proven expertise in managing complex problems in multi-layered organizations. Has gained rapid promotion as a result of a determined approach and a progressive attitude to finding new solutions. A team player, comfortable with responsibility and keen to rise to opportunities, Stephen is available to join a lively team working in an organization where he can contribute to the full.

ACHIEVEMENTS:
▧ Increased profits in present post by 50 per cent over five years.
▧ Spearheading new ways of working through Knowledge Management.
▧ Successfully completed demanding Management Trainee programme.
▧ Obtained promotion after impressing senior managers in my first post.
▧ Wide range of interests outside work that involve team collaboration.

RELEVANT EXPERIENCE:
▧ Team Leader, Ford Brothers (2006 to date) – running Business Strategy team of seven, spearheading business decisions for the company. The business grew or shrank directly according to the decisions we took. The last five years have shown a steady increase in profits. Reporting directly to the Director of Sales and Strategy, recently developing new discipline of Knowledge Management for the company.

■ Management Trainee, Appledore Analysis (2002–2005) – achieved consistently high marks for endeavour and creative problem solving on this one-year programme.** Specialized in using and developing new systems for improving project management across a wide range of applications. Promoted to Supervisor at the end of year.

EDUCATION:

2001	Charter College	BA Degree and
	Godalming	a Diploma in
		Management Studies

INTERESTS:
A wide range of spare-time activities including windsailing in the summer, rugby in the winter, team running all year round and playing the piano with a musical group.

CONTACT:
Stephen Deery
14 Camberwell Road
Fentown
Warwickshire
CU3 9OP

Tel: 01200 000000
E-mail: deery339045@example.com

REFERENCES:

Tom Perks	Joanne Stacey
Director of Sales and Strategy	Personnel Director
Appledore Analysis	Ford Brothers
Fentown	Wentforth
Warwickshire	Warwickshire
CU3 9LK	CU14 2NN
Tel 01200 100000	Tel: 01289 000000
E-mail: perks@example.com	E-mail: joannes@example.com

> * Try this style of CV with the personal profile at the top to see if you
> like the way it looks.
> ** Highlight any achievements that you were responsible for.

Stephen's CV is written in an up-front style and it is a style that is becoming more common in the UK too. It starts with a definite and bold statement about his experience, achievements and qualities. This paragraph is aimed at 'selling' this jobseeker as someone worth taking note of. The advantage of this style is that the highlights are presented unapologetically right at the start of the document. It is saying: 'Look, this is what I have to offer – are you interested?' In more modern, international or sales-oriented businesses, the employers will be used to this kind of document. They will be happy to look at the first paragraph and decide whether or not to read more based on whether they like what they see there. No time is wasted if there is not a match between what the applicant is offering and the kind of person that the employer is looking for.

However, this also illustrates the slight disadvantages of this kind of CV. If it is presented to a more traditional, local or public sector organization, the employer may be put off by the slightly more unusual 'take me or leave me' uncompromising tone. The hard sell will not be as successful here as the more gradual or gentle approach adopted in all the examples given previously. The format recommended there leads the reader in to the document by highlighting the writer's relevant education and experience. The format is more conservative but the advantage is that it will put fewer people off and could encourage more employers to dig deeper to find out more about the applicant.

Experiment with your own CV, putting it into different types of layout. See which you think is best and try different versions on different employers to check if one has a greater success rate.

13. Hybrid (Version 1)

CV HOLLY ENTWHISTLE

394 Central Parade
Longfield
N Yorkshire YO3 IXC

Tel: 01911 000 000
E-mail: holent@example.com

PROFILE:*
A self-motivated and creative manager, Holly has had 12 years' experience of leading teams in customer relations. She understands how to handle the range of customers' experience with products and services and her many achievements show the difference that she can make. Her calm attitude and skills with people ensure she offers a unique contribution to an organization that is driven by its customers' opinions.

ACHIEVEMENTS:
▓ Increased customer satisfaction.
In each role I have worked hard to increase customer satisfaction with the company. This sounds simple but involves giving detailed attention to a complex set of relationships and transactions, making sure that each one is as effective as possible.

▓ Reduced level of complaints.
In my present job, the level of complaints now stands at a record low level. I devised a plan to reorganize the way that complaints from customers are handled and this has revolutionized the whole customer care strategy for the organization.

▓ Greater team productivity.
Customer relations go well if the team dealing with this area are motivated and efficient. I take a pride in the high ratings I have always received from my team in my regular 360-degree appraisal. My team rate me as firm but fair and know I am always open to hearing their point of view.

TRAINING:
I believe in lifelong learning.** After a good general education and leaving college with a BTEC in Business Studies, I have continued my training through many short courses offered through the workplace. Over the last 10 years these include: advanced customer care, supervisory skills, motivating and leading effective teams, health and safety at work, personal image, and career development and planning.

OTHER SKILLS AND INTERESTS:
I do regular sponsored walks for a charity I support – and this activity keeps me fit. I sing in a local choir and we give public performances from time to time. This always makes me nervous but I rise to the challenge on the day. I enjoy going to the theatre and the cinema fairly frequently.

REFERENCES:
Rohini Truelove
Managing Director
Westcare Ltd
Stapley Business Centre
South Street
Hobbleton
Yorks
YO9 1UU

Tel: 01773 000000
E-mail: rtruelove@example.com

Cllr Kevin Didcot
Yately Health Authority
Southwold Civic Centre
Yately
Oxon
OX3 3PL

Tel: 01998 000000
E-mail: didcot@example.com

> * This profile is written in the third person ('Holly has ...'), rather than the first person ('I have ...').
>
> ** Don't just list your courses – explain more about your attitude to training and learning.

In reality, many people produce a document that takes parts of different styles and mixes them to produce a hybrid, or individually composed, CV that they feel most comfortable with. The example above illustrates this kind of layout.

Holly has written one of these CVs. She is mixing and matching layouts to produce a document that she feels will increase her chances of success. She uses the opening 'selling' paragraph that we saw in the last example, although the tone is slightly more gentle here. She has decided to lay out her work experience as a series of achievements relevant to the kind of job she is seeking, rather than just listing her chronological posts.

She summarizes her education and training to highlight those areas that will be of particular interest to employers and shows her varied interests outside work. She has used a more unusual font to present her CV in the hope that this will add to its attractiveness.

Once you have composed your CV, it is easy to experiment with different styles of presentation.

14. Hybrid (Version 2)

Melody LEWIS – CV
9 Pennery Road
NORTH CHEADLE
Suffolk
IP3 3LL

Tel: 02252 00000
Mobile: 07794 00000
E-mail: m.lewis@example.com

Personal profile: *
An experienced and trustworthy team player, I have used my experience at work to build my abilities and widen my knowledge. I make a difference by forging a positive and harmonious atmosphere through my people skills and am able to motivate others in a group setting. I am a determined person who has great stamina for the long haul. Learning on the job is important to me and has enabled me to contribute fully to the success of the busy legal firm where I work.

Education and training:
I left school in 1999 with six GCSEs including English and Maths.

I have been on several vocational courses with my present employer including:

■ health and safety;
■ public speaking;
■ having impact in the workplace;
■ networking;
■ general computing courses.

I attend evening classes to keep my learning up to date. At the moment I am studying Spanish and this has proved to be useful at work with some of our European clients.

Employment:
For the last 10 years I have worked for Cheadle Law, a firm of solicitors. I joined after leaving school in 1999 as a clerical assistant and have been promoted twice, first to team leader and then to office manager. My responsibilities include all aspects of running the general office and keeping client accounts. I work as the supervisor of four other people and we work well as a considerate and effective team. Being an ambassador is a role which comes naturally as I like meeting new people. I am often asked to represent the firm at conferences and events and am known as the friendly face of the company locally.

Interests:
There is a regional law association of which our company is a member. I am the link person for this association in my firm and as a committee member I help to run the programme of lectures and presentations which are held each year. Outside work, I am a member of a choir and we give local concerts each year. I enjoy camping with friends on holiday and have recently started training as a pilates fitness instructor.**

References:
Character reference:
Dr Jacob Riley GP
93 Starling Close
London
NW4 8KT

Tel: 020 8447 6221
E-mail: jriley@example.com

Reference available from my present employer on request.

* This profile is written in the first person ('I have ...'). But try not to start every sentence with 'I ...', or it becomes boring.
** The wider the range of interests you include, the more dynamic you sound.

Melody has chosen her own way of presenting her background to make the most impact she can. She is relying on her character to get her a place at an interview rather than extensive job experience or a long list of qualifications. She does not use the traditional layout but mixes the styles to describe herself in a way with which she feels comfortable.

She has worked with the same company for the last 10 years. She makes the most of her experience there by starting with a punchy personal profile to convey her strengths, primarily as a team player and middle manager. Melody has had considerable training since she left school, which will be relevant to any new job application, so she discusses all her education and training together.

Her interests are varied and the fact that she helps run a professional association will catch an employer's eye. She does not want her present employer to be approached for a reference unless she is contacted to take her application further.

15. Hybrid (Version 3)

CV – Andrew CRUICKSHANK*
83 Melbourne Grove
ACKLEY
Ayrshire
AY5 7HB

Tel: 08831 000 000
Mobile: 07652 000 000
E-mail: acruickshank@example.com

Nationality: British

Employment history:
Company General Manager, Firewall Plus, Ackley, 2000 to date
Firewall Plus is a specialist marble flooring company with a high profile in the interior design industry. I work alongside three directors and oversee all aspects of the business and manage 35 employees.

Management responsibilities:

▓ Property: Managing leases of our property portfolio, liaison with landlords and tenants.

▓ Projects: Liaising with contractors and keeping contracts on budget and to time.

▓ Finances: Evaluation and monitoring of the financial affairs of the company including purchasing and leasing arrangements.

▓ Corporate affairs: Developing the internal organization to aid reaching business objectives.

▓ External affairs: Managing events and marketing promotions, improving the visual image of the company.

▓ Legal work: Ensure compliance with pertinent legislation, promoting corporate responsibility in all areas of our work.

▓ Personnel management: Recruiting and managing all new staff, appraising and mentoring a large team and developing work schedules.

During 2002 I had a series of temporary administrative jobs.

Education:
A Levels in Government & Politics and English, 1998
BSc (Hons) Degree in Quantity Surveying at Luton University, 2001

Other skills/abilities:**

- Computer literacy: Word and Excel, Sage, experience with Apple Macs.
- Good knowledge of French and German.
- Qualified first aider.
- Own car and have a clean, full driving licence.

Interests:
I have been a parent governor and vice-chair of the governing body at my child's nursery school for three years. This has taught me a great deal about the way equal opportunities and special needs are incorporated into the curriculum for very young children. I help out with a local theatre company and I have also been a theatre assessor for Scottish Arts for two years.

I am a member of a reading group where we share, analyse and interpret good books. I am a keen amateur piano player and am shortly to take my Grade Four exam. I travel around the UK visiting Norman sites and buildings, an interest that started after visiting the Bayeux Tapestry in France and learning about William the Conqueror.

Other information:
I am an enthusiastic, experienced and approachable manager. Making the time to understand staff is important and pays dividends in getting the best from all members of the team.

I have a highly-developed attention to detail, with excellent planning skills, sound commercial awareness and a 'can-do' attitude to problems and challenges at work. I make the most of new technology and enjoy turning information into knowledge.***

I consider myself to be a well-rounded person, enjoying life both inside and outside my work.

References: Available on request.

* You can choose to put your identifying details in the centre, as Andrew has done, or on the left-hand side, as in the previous example.
** Use bullet points and lists where you can, to vary your presentation.
*** Use dynamic, upbeat words to make your CV stand out from the pile.

Andrew has a senior job with a lot of responsibility for the well-being of the company. However, apart from some short-term work in 2002, this is his only job since leaving college so he is keen to show just how important his role at work is.

He feels that there is more to him than just being a good manager. He thinks his outside interests will be of interest so he takes the time to explain about them here.

He uses a combination of styles, starting with placing the focus on the main tasks of his present job which he thinks will be his major selling point. He then moves on to his education and then his other skills and interests. He uses the 'Other information' section to further explain how his personality and character could be an asset to a new employer.

6

Preparing your own CV

Step-by-step guide

Many points have been made in this book about the best way to prepare your own CV. It can seem daunting actually to get going when your head is full of all the possibilities. But it is important for your career that you make a start on preparing or updating your own document. The best time to do this is before there is an urgent need for you to have your CV ready – you need to devote enough time to its preparation to ensure that you do yourself justice. It is much more difficult to do this if you are in a big rush.

Bad luck and lack of planning will often cause the time you need to prepare your CV in a hurry to coincide with another event. It could be that your single remaining printer ink runs out after all the shops have shut, or you develop a hideous illness that stops you working, or you experience a domestic emergency that drives all thoughts of job searching out of your mind. Let's get going straight away while you are able to and with the advice in this book fresh in your mind.

Writing a CV does not happen all in one go. You start by making an initial attempt at the document. You can then correct this draft – editing and improving it with each new version until you reach one that you feel is as good as you can make it.

Once you start putting things down on paper, you will find that you begin to get involved in the process of creating this 'story of your life'. Writing something that you will be proud of will be a satisfying piece of work.

This section takes you step by step through the key points to recap on what has been suggested. Reading this chapter should help you to remember what has been said before and encourage you to focus on the key points for action. Getting started can be the hardest part of all, but, once you get going, you will find that the challenge of producing an impressive document seems easier straight away once you have taken your first steps.

Step 1: Drafting your CV

Start the process of preparing your own CV by putting together a draft or rough version. Do this work at a time when you can put yourself into a positive frame of mind, and in a place where you can think creatively and work on presenting yourself in the best light. Choose a quiet time and place where you will not be disturbed, as you will need all of your concentration for the task. Using a large sheet of paper or the blank form at the end of this chapter on page 131, start to fill in all the sections, beginning with your personal details, through to your referees. Refer to Chapter 3 to help you to complete each section.

You are now working on your first draft of your CV. It will not emerge as the perfect model for some time, so do not get bogged down in detail at this point. In your first go at writing this document you should not hold back. At this stage you want to put in all the information that you can remember. Cover as much ground as you can concerning your background. If you have never written a CV before, you may find this part trickier as you will have to check back for accuracy about where, when and what you worked at and studied. However, once you have researched this information from your past for yourself, you will have it recorded for any purpose in the future.

Education

Starting from your secondary education (age 11 onwards), include every school and college attended, each course studied and all qualifications gained. You can sift and evaluate this information later on, but it is easier to decide to leave material out than to find out that you do not have enough to include. Take yourself back to those days and try to think back to the time you spent at each of these places. Include notes on any particular achievements or highlights that you remember.

Employment

Move on now to note down every employer that you have ever worked for, whether it was full- or part-time, permanent or temporary, holiday or voluntary work. This represents the essential raw material from which will come the finished version of your CV. You will not want to include every possible detail in the real thing but writing them down in rough will help you to decide what to use later on. Try to be as accurate as possible with the relevant dates and facts. Refer back to old payslips and other work documents to get these right.

You need to include the dates when you worked at each place – just the month and year – together with the name and location of each workplace and the main activities of each job. If you had any particular achievements or successes in the job, note them down too.

Other skills

Rack your brains for things to add to this section. Driving licence, first aid, computer and word-processing skills would all fit in here. There may be some particular skills that are relevant to the job you are applying for that you have not been able to include elsewhere, such as using certain tools, machinery or equipment. Language ability should be mentioned in this part of the document. There may be specific practical training courses that you have attended that fit into this section, eg computer courses, customer care, sales and marketing or management.

We want to include anything you know about, or have been taught, that does not naturally fit into the education part of your CV.

Interests

For this draft CV, include any pastimes or hobbies that you have ever spent time on, to give you a list from which to choose three or four sporty pursuits; then write down the same number of activities which show your other interests. The more you can show that you are an 'all-rounder', the better. Include interests that show you can use your brain as well as your hands and those that illustrate that you enjoy team involvement as well as solo work. Try to include something creative too.

Take this section seriously as it can really help to enliven your CV. What is it that makes you choose this as a pastime? What have you done with regard to this activity? Are you a beginner or have you moved on with the subject? How do you want to develop in this area?

Additional information

Do not be tempted to miss out this section. If your CV is merely a list of places you have worked and studied, you will be missing a real opportunity. Explaining effectively what kind of person you are can prove to be a winner in the race to get your CV noticed. Whether you choose to have this section as a 'personal profile' paragraph at the start of your CV or include it as an 'additional information' section later on, you need to describe your personality so that any reader can imagine you in person to see if you would fit in the vacancy on offer.

This is the section where you can really go to town. If you want your CV to jump out at an employer, use this space to pick out your particular strengths. Just write down what your best friend, or perhaps your mother, would say about you – on a good day! How would they describe your best points to an employer? Go back and complete the exercise on pages 39–40 to help you think of things to write here.

Don't worry about sounding boastful. This is the only information that employers will have to go on, so this section is telling them that they should definitely invite you for an interview. Remember only to talk about what you have to offer. Illustrate what you think you can contribute in the right position. Create two paragraphs as a minimum here.

References

Include two referees who will help create a good impression about you. Check with both your referees that they are quite happy to be included in your CV. Make sure that their details are correct and include full and current contact details including their e-mail addresses.

You may not want to include referees in your CV, but if this is the case, you must ensure that you have two people on whom you can call at short notice to provide references for you quickly. If employers want to take up your references, they will not want to wait for you to find two suitable people, so you need to be sure that you have up-to-date details ready to be provided at all times once you send your CV to anyone. You may be one of many possibly suitable candidates and any unnecessary delay may mean that you get crossed off the list.

Step 2: Editing your CV

Take a break from the writing work you have done. Doing something else for a short while before returning to carry on with your CV will refresh you and help you look at your work more objectively. When you are ready, sit down and prepare to start editing your work.

Now read everything you have written down so far and decide what to include or delete. You will need to spend the most time on the 'Education' and 'Employment' sections. The rule here is – if in doubt, leave it out, so the only information that remains is clear, concise and interesting to read. It must tell the story of your studies and career to date, stressing your achievements and showing your development.

Look through the examples in Chapter 5 to see the sort of information that other people have included in their CVs. Look at each section of your draft document and try to think what needs to be included to give a fair picture of your experience. This step can only be done by you, but remember that the whole CV should only cover two or three sheets of A4 paper; you will not have room for anything but the essential information. Ask yourself 'Does this part of the CV add to the total impression?' before you leave it in. Be alert to the need to update regularly the terms you use. The 'world wide web' is now usually referred to as the 'internet'. Words change over time and you do not want to appear to be out of touch. Check also the kind of words you are using. Moderate words will appear mediocre, so exchange them for bolder, bigger language, eg 'achieved', 'successful', 'maximized', 'enjoy', 'relish', 'satisfaction'.

Getting feedback

It is always helpful to get direct feedback on how your document appears to someone else.

At this stage, enlist a friend or relative to take an objective look at what you have written. He or she may be able to tell you if some information needs to be made clearer, or if some parts of the CV are too long or too short. He or she may also be able to spot mistakes that you have completely missed. Leave the document for a couple of days, and then return to it to evaluate again if it is creating the impression you are looking for. Consider if you want to vary the layout or if you are happy that the traditional format is the best one for your purposes. See Chapter 5 for alternatives.

Step 3: The final version

Now check through everything you have written. If you are sure it is all correct and accurate, then you are ready to get the final version properly laid out.

However good the person is who types your CV, you must make sure that you check and re-check the document for accuracy of content and attractive presentation. If your CV is produced on a computer, it will be a fairly simple matter to make corrections; time spent proof-reading at this stage will save having to hurry later on.

Once the document has been typed, print a copy and show it to somebody else. Another person will often be able to spot errors that you will blank out, however many times you reread it.

If you now feel happy that your CV is a good representation of your strengths and assets, the real test is to use it to apply for jobs and to contact employers.

Step 4: The covering letter

Unless you are completing your document online, you will never send out your CV on its own. You always need to accompany it with a covering letter to the employer. At the very least you will write a letter saying which job you are applying for.

Even if a covering letter has not been specifically requested, it is another opportunity to explain more about yourself. As such this letter can be a great additional asset to your application. Many people leave it at just stating which vacancy they are interested in and do not exploit the opportunity available through effective use of the letter. It gives you the chance to attract the reader's attention by restating your strengths and to have another go at showing what contribution you could make to the job. Think of the effect of the letter on your CV in the same way as the cover of a book. It grabs the reader's attention, highlights what is interesting inside, and attracts the reader to read on and find out more. A good letter can help your CV go to the top of the shortlisted pile of those to be interviewed.

What goes in a covering letter?

In most cases you will need to say why you are sending your CV, tell the employer a little about yourself and what you want to happen next. A letter one to two pages in length can help to answer the one question on any employer's mind: what contribution can you make to this company or organization?

Go back to the list of your best qualities that you used for the 'additional information' section and reiterate the key points in a different form in your letter. Obviously all letters will be personal to the writer, but here are some general hints about the way to put your covering letter together:

- Keep the letter reasonably brief – the employer has already got two pages of your CV to read. The letter should never be longer than two sides of A4 paper.

- This is your introduction to your CV – make sure your letter is interesting enough for your CV to be actually read. Think of this letter as a sales document. Use short sentences and positive words to create a memorable and attractive effect.

- Always be very courteous – it costs you nothing and politeness cannot help but impress the reader.

- Use new, unlined writing paper to create a good impression. Use a computer to write the covering letter. Handwriting is much more unusual these days. If it must be handwritten ensure it is *extremely* neat. Use the same type of paper as you did for the CV if possible, so they match.

- Take as much care over the letter as you have with your CV. Your hard work on the CV may be wasted if the employer takes a dislike to a hasty or messy letter, and throws the lot into the waste-paper bin.

- If you are sending your CV in response to an advertisement, make sure that you address the letter to the correct person, and say where you saw the vacancy. The company may be advertising several jobs at the same time, in different publications, and will need to know which one you are applying for.

- If this is a speculative letter, it always stands more chance of success if it is addressed to someone in particular. So if you are approaching employers who may have vacancies, but who have not yet advertised, try to find out the name of the person you want to approach and address the letter to him or her personally.

▨ Shrug off the worry that your letter sounds boastful. It needs to be larger than life to get you noticed.

▨ Attach the letter to your CV with a paperclip so it does not get separated.

Examples of covering letters

Helen Guyer
99 Green Street
Carlisle
CL2 0LB

15 December 2009

Ms Charnley
White Brothers
Longfields Estate
Carlisle
CL1 9OP

Tel: 05800 700 000
E-mail: hguyer@example.com

Dear Ms Charnley

I enclose my curriculum vitae for your attention. I am a 31-year-old mother of two children. As you can see from my CV, I have five years' experience of clerical work in a busy office* and have recently completed a computing course at a local training centre.

I thoroughly enjoy working in administration and I know that unless the paperwork is accurate any company will suffer. Therefore I am careful about checking important details and always help my colleagues out to get the work done.

I am highly motivated, ambitious and enjoy working to deadlines. I have excellent references and would relish the chance to work as part of the team at White Brothers.

I should be grateful if you would contact me if you have any vacancies in your company, or keep my information on file in case of future openings.

Thank you for your attention in this matter. I look forward to hearing from you.

Yours sincerely

Helen Guyer

Helen Guyer

---

* Helen highlights her previous experience.

Mr Chris Blackfoot
889 Croxted Drive
LONDON
SE18 0RM
E-mail: blackfoot@example.com

23 November 2009

Mr John Schumacher
Director
OGA
15 Shawshank Buildings
Fallowfield Crescent
LONDON
SW2 9PZ

Dear Mr Schumacher,

Further to our phone conversation today, I am writing in case you have a relevant vacancy in the near future. As you can see from my CV, my current position is Director of Finance in a leading insurance company. I have worked at ABC Insurance for the last six years and started as financial controller there before being promoted to head the directorate three years ago.

I enjoy dealing with strategic issues and take a full part in running the organization with the rest of the leadership of ABC Insurance. I work with a large, highly motivated team who understand their crucial role in the fortunes of the company. Last year I was the company's internal project leader in our successful application for the Investors in People standard.*

I am now looking to move into the charity sector and am happy to forgo the financial benefits of the private sector in order to make a full contribution to an organization like OGA. International health issues have interested me since I was a student and I am highly motivated to be part of your organization, which is making a real difference in this field.

I would be keen to meet to discuss any aspect of my CV if you felt there was a vacancy which I might suit. Many thanks for your time.

Best regards,

Chris Blackfoot

Chris Blackfoot

* Chris outlines his achievements in his last job.

Step 5

Now carefully save a copy of your CV and covering letter, both on computer and on paper, if possible. Together with the details of which jobs you have applied for, this forms a vital record of those employers you approach, or positions you apply for. Staple the sheets of your CV together, use a paperclip to add on the letter, and use a big enough envelope so you don't need to fold the CV.

If you send out your CV and do not get a reply, it is always worth ringing the company in a couple of weeks' time, to check if there is any news. Following up politely in this way can help you eliminate those employers who are definitely not interested.

Conclusion

Your CV is a tool for job-seeking purposes. Like any other tool, its value lies in the manner in which you use it. Keep abreast of the way the world of work is changing. Be interested in articles about what employers are looking for. Use your CV if you are looking for work. Make sure friends in the same line of work have a copy. Get opinions from others about how effective a document they believe it to be. Look at other people's examples to see how they have compiled theirs.

Think of this CV of yours as a living, breathing organism that requires feeding to keep it operating at peak efficiency. If you are in work, your CV needs updating with every new job, appraisal, training course, promotion or change in your responsibilities. If you start new interests or experience achievements in work, education or voluntary work, add these. If you develop your personality in a new direction or get different positive feedback from a manager about yourself, enhance the 'Additional information' section or personal profile straight away. If you change your mind about your career direction, draft another version of your CV in case you find an opportunity to develop in this area.

Dos and don'ts

✔ Do experiment with different fonts, layouts and contents of your CV, but remember to keep it simple, straightforward and clear, whichever you choose.

✔ Do reject any information that does not enhance your impact with employers, and keep evaluating your CV to ensure it stays the best it can be.

✔ Do take as much care with a covering letter so that your CV gets the chance to do its work on your behalf.

✗ Don't leave your CV to moulder in a drawer and then find you are caught unawares with a document that needs a lot of work.

✗ Don't take rejection personally; there may just have been a more suitable person for the position this time.

✗ Don't give up if you are knocked back – the right job could be just around the next corner.

Points to remember

1. Work hard to produce a document of which you feel proud.

2. The best time to do work on your CV is when you do not need it urgently.

3. A meek outline of your strengths is not enough, so boast!

4. Use different versions of your CV if you feel different career directions warrant it.

5. A good covering letter can boost your chance of success.

Good luck!

Blank CV

CURRICULUM VITAE

(NAME)

(ADDRESS)

(Tel:)
(E-mail:)

EDUCATION:

(Dates)   (Name and location)   (Qualifications or subjects
studied)

EMPLOYMENT:

(Dates)   (Name and location)   (Position held and main
duties)

OTHER SKILLS:

INTERESTS:

ADDITIONAL INFORMATION:

REFERENCES:

7

Using the internet

Using the internet to help you prepare your CV

There are many sites on the internet that give you assistance with compiling a CV. Most are sites displaying job vacancies. They make their money from recruitment advertising from employers or by taking a commission from companies if they place you in a job. As part of the information they provide around searching for jobs, these sites often include tips on CVs, interview skills and other career development issues. Jobseekers can access these pages free of charge, although, if you want to use their specialized targeting process for locating the most relevant jobs to suit you, you may be required to go through a registration process.

Many sites exist either to help you compile a full CV (companies usually charge for this service) or to distribute a shorter free version on your behalf to targeted companies. Known as an 'online CV', this is a CV produced to a formula layout that can be quickly completed and distributed on your behalf. Essentially, completing an online CV is a matter of filling in the boxes on the screen in front of you to create lists of your experience, qualifications and abilities. These CVs are therefore not personally designed documents.

Free services could well be worth sampling in case they bring up new contacts. Be careful though about paying money online for a service of this kind, unless you are sure that the benefits will be worth it. Try to talk to people who have used the service before you spend money on it. A scrappy formulaic CV sent as junk mail along with many others to unwilling recipients may not enhance your chances of success.

Applying for jobs online

Many organizations now recruit directly through the internet. They assess application forms and CVs that have been sent in to their organization or they search specialized recruitment sites to find applicants who might be suitable for their vacancies. It is both cheaper and quicker for companies to accept online applications. They do not have to pay a recruitment agency and they (and you) can access the applications any time of the day.

Do not be scared of using the internet as a method of posting your CV to employers. It can be a powerful way of getting yourself in front of employers and shows you can handle new technology. For some jobs it is now the main way to apply – in the IT sector, for example. Overall, around two-thirds of all employers accept online applications as part of their recruitment process.

Electronic application and selection methods mean that your document may look different at its destination from the way it did when you e-mailed it. It may also change again when dealt with, copied or scanned at the employer's premises. This means that applications for this kind of delivery need to be constructed and presented in a way that takes account of how they will be sent, received and processed.

Using keywords

Employers can receive hundreds of forms electronically. They use computer programs to help them deal with this.

When recruiters search through CVs electronically they will do so by looking for keywords in each document. So what are keywords? Recruiters identify certain trigger words that they feel should be covered by candidates who stand a chance of being successful for their vacancy. Keywords tend to be nouns describing the kind of work applicants have done in the past that will be directly relevant to the job on offer, eg:

▦ management;	▦ accounting;
▦ administration;	▦ project leadership;
▦ organization;	▦ training;
▦ supervision;	▦ human resources.

Or else they refer to the name of the position held, eg:

▦ manager;	▦ project manager;
▦ administrator;	▦ technician;
▦ supervisor;	▦ team leader.

Or they refer to the name of the specific skill or knowledge required, eg:

▦ Word;	▦ budget management;
▦ Excel;	▦ information technology;
▦ PowerPoint;	▦ accounting software.

You can see how these keywords are similar to the transferable skills required by an employer, just specified by single words that identify the key skills and attributes concerned.

Employers searching by keywords will select any CV for further consideration that mentions a critical number of the keywords identified. Furthermore they may want certain words to be given a high priority by the successful candidates. If you leave the fact that you have managed teams to the last paragraph in your CV, you may not get selected to be interviewed for a relevant position where managing staff is a priority task.

Identifying the keywords that may be used for a job that interests you will mean that you have to do some thinking and researching about the job. A close examination of the job description and person specification will enable you to spot the keywords used by the recruiter about the job. If it is a type of employment that you are already familiar with, think about the many topical words that get used often with that kind of business and try to incorporate the most familiar into this version of your CV. If it is a new work area that you are trying to break into, research through professional journals, talking to people in the business and closely examining adverts for similar positions to discover the keywords that frequently occur. Make sure you pay close attention to the particular words and phrases the recruiter uses to describe the vacancy, as these will often be the same keywords they expect to see in your CV.

Scannable CVs

Some employers accept paper CVs and then scan them into a recruitment software package. This reads the CV and prioritizes it by matching it by keywords. Scanners cannot always read bold or italic print, so a plain layout for your CV is recommended if you know it is likely to be scanned on receipt. Any CV that is longer than one page is unlikely to be dealt with so keep your CV brief if you know it is likely to be scanned – leave out the less relevant parts of your full version, such as interests.

Electronic CVs

In order for your CV to be instantly readable by any package that may receive it, you need to write and save it in the lowest common denominator of formats. Plain text format is the most common internet format. Keep bullet points simple, just as you do in e-mails.

▩ Set the margins at 6.5 inches.

▩ Write in Courier 12 point so that you get 65 characters per line of text.

▩ Write with no bold, underlining or italics so that your document can be interpreted in any package.

▩ Do not use fancy graphics as this may not be clear on receipt.

▩ Save as a 'text only' document when prompted how you wish to save it.

▩ Check it in a text editor such as Notepad in Windows to see how it will look to an employer on receipt.

▩ Add at the end that you can also provide the document in whatever format you normally use, eg Word.

E-mailing your CV

The e-mail that you attach to your CV should include the same content as a covering letter for a CV that you post. Attach the CV both in Word and as a text file for ease of viewing.

Filling in an online application form or e-form

This is an electronic version of an application form that requires you to input text into specific boxes, or fields, and then send this information to the employer's or recruiter's website. If the questions tally, you can copy and paste information direct from the text version of your CV.

CV banks

Some websites exist just to hold online CVs in a data bank, which can then be accessed by employers looking for candidates. You may have to pay for this service but you may find that it is an effective way of finding out about new vacancies if you have impressive previous experience and transferable skills. You will often be asked to input a geographical area within which you would be interested in working.

Useful sites

Some sites specialize in recruitment, others feature a recruitment page and company or organization sites may also show vacancies within that organization. Some sites work as online recruitment agencies, allowing you to lodge your details with them in the form of your CV. Employers know they can search through the CVs held online to look for suitable candidates.

Security

Think carefully about where and how you post your CV online. If it is an open site with easy access by employers, you may find that your current boss sees that you are searching around for a new job. Would this be a problem for you?

Dos and don'ts

✔ Do update your CV regularly on jobsearch websites and in CV banks so that, if employers only want to see the most recent, yours will be near the top of the pile.

✔ Do always include full contact details and your e-mail address.

✔ Do spend time getting the correct keywords in your CV. Examine carefully all the information you can about the employer and the vacancy concerned. Look too at other details for similar jobs at the right level. Use all the significant nouns that describe the key activities in the job or the characteristics required.

✗ Don't apply for more than one job in one company. It will look as though you are applying indiscriminately because you are desperate.

✗ Don't just sit back and wait after you have applied online. You still need to be conducting other job search activities in case you have no success from this approach.

✗ Don't think because you are applying online that presentation is less important. It is just as important but different methods need to be used to make sure you create the best impression.

Points to remember

1. Many more employers are using online recruitment to save themselves time and money. It is now the standard way to recruit for jobs in some sectors.

2. It is more work to prepare your CV to be accessed online but it could increase your chances of being picked out by an employer.

3. Only attempt to send an online CV if you have ensured that it will be an impressive document once received by the employer.

4. You still need to find out all you can about the organization to help you present the most impressive application you can and to make your CV stand out from the crowd.

5. Never dash off an online CV – it will be paid as much attention as any other application, so take your time to prepare it thoroughly.

10 great sites for jobseekers

The internet is a fast-changing scene and new sites appear as fast as others fall from view. Here are 10 of the current best for UK jobseekers:

1. www.timesonline.co.uk
   The website of the *Times* newspaper group, which contains their jobs pages. It is particularly useful for senior vacancies and managerial, technical and senior secretarial positions. This site includes CV tips and guidelines, topical interview advice and career development articles.

2. www.prospects.ac.uk
   Labelled as 'the UK's official graduate careers website', this site is provided by the Higher Education Careers Services Unit. Accessible and functional, this is a useful resource for graduates and, by gathering all the key points together, can help to focus graduate job search or paths to further study. Articles give pointers to compiling a CV and there is extensive job search information and advice here.

3. www.jobs.guardian.co.uk
   'The UK's most popular newspaper website', provided by the *Guardian* newspaper group, which owns the national newspaper with the largest selection of jobs. This site is accessible and impressive, and is easy to search for jobs by relevance to your needs. It has many new jobs every day, listed by broad sector and seniority so is worth checking on a regular basis for national-level jobs. You can complete a profile on this site to which your CV can be attached. This electronic document can then be made available to specific employers who may be interested in you. There is no charge for this service. You can also upload your CV so that it can be sent to any vacancy that interests you.

4. www.ft.com
   This is the recruitment site provided by the *Financial Times* newspaper. It includes job vacancies, particularly in the financial sector and has some job search tips.

5. www.jobs.co.uk
   This site links to employers' websites so that you can apply for a job directly.

6. www.targetjobs.co.uk
   A commercial jobsearch site with many vacancies.

7. www.reed.co.uk
   This site is owned by Reed employment, a leading agency. It includes recruitment career tips including CV advice and interview techniques.

8. www.bradleycvs.co.uk
   This website is produced by a company that offers a CV writing service for a fee. The site is useful, offering free information on compiling a CV and examples of CVs. It also has articles on job search skills including interview techniques. This site has many links to other specific recruitment sites.

9. www.monster.co.uk
   A commercial recruitment website with extensive job search advice included.

10. www.jobsgopublic.com
    A public sector jobs website.

Other useful sites

General vacancy sites

www.jobs1.co.uk
www.jobtrack.co.uk
www.peoplebank.co.uk
www.stepstone.co.uk
www.topjobs.co.uk
www.ukjobs.com

CV writing and posting

www.cvspecial.co.uk

Voluntary opportunities sites

www.jobseekers.direct.gov.uk
This is the UK government's portal to all sorts of jobs, training and volunteering opportunities. Just click on 'voluntary work' and input your postcode or the kind of work you would like to do, to see what is available.

www.jobcentreplus.gov.uk
The UK government's jobs website has information on voluntary opportunities.

www.volunteering.org.uk
Run by Volunteering England, this site has a wealth of opportunities to share.

www.do-it.org.uk
This is a national database of volunteering opportunities run by YouthNet, a national charity. It collects details from volunteer centres around the UK to publicize what is available.

Other sites

Jobcentre Plus: www.jobcentreplus.gov.uk
Royal British Legion (ex-servicemen and women): www.rbli.co.uk
General business directory: www.ukbusinesspark.co.uk
Confederation of British Industry: www.cbi.org.uk
Listing of recruitment agencies: www.ipl.co.uk/recruit.html

Newspaper and publishers' sites

TES: www.jobs.tes.co.uk
Telegraph: www.jobs.telegraph.co.uk
Evening Standard (London vacancies): www.londonjobs.co.uk
Summary of local newspapers' jobs: www.fish4.co.uk/iad/jobs

Other sources of help

Learn Direct Helpline

The Learn Direct number, 0800 101 901, is a UK-Government funded telephone helpline available to everyone. Ring the freephone number and you will be given advice about local sources of help on careers and learning issues. This could include where to contact the types of organizations mentioned below. Visit the comprehensive website for advice, help and information at www.learndirect.co.uk.

The Connexions Service

In some areas of the country, the staff in your local Connexions Service can offer help and advice to adults, although their main client group is 16–19-year-olds. They will have reference books about employers and applying for jobs, and understanding, skilled staff who can help you put your CV together if you get stuck. Find the telephone number in the local phone book and ring them to speak to a personal adviser to find out more. Their website is www.connexions-direct.com. Visit the website for a huge database of careers information at www.connexions-direct.com/jobs4u, which can tell you about any job you have an interest in.

Jobcentre Plus

The UK's Jobcentre Plus network is government funded and carries job vacancies and can offer access to help with jobsearch skills and retraining if you are unemployed. The website is at: www.jobcentreplus.gov.uk.

Careers advice

The UK government funds a careers advice site to offer information and help with decision making and jobsearch skills. They have a comprehensive website at: www.careersadvice. direct.gov.uk. If you need to talk to an adviser, you can ring their advice line on 0800 101 901.

Recruitment agencies

Agencies may wish to compile a CV for you for a particular type of job to help them to 'sell' you to an employer. They charge the employer if you are placed with a company and you will not always be allowed to have a copy of the CV they compile for your own use.

Private careers counsellors

You can get help from careers counsellors who work privately and who make a charge for their service. This can be very expensive and although they will help you to put the CV together and then print it out on a top quality printer, you will also be charged extra for any reprints and amendments that you may require in the future.

Further reading from Kogan Page

Interview and Career Guidance

A to Z of Careers and Jobs, 16th edition, Susan Hodgson, 2009
Careers after the Armed Forces, Jon Mitchell, 2009
Careers and Jobs in IT, David Yardley, 2004
Careers and Jobs in the Media, Simon Kent, 2005
Careers and Jobs in Nursing, Linda Nazarko, 2004
Careers and Jobs in the Police Service, Kim Clabby, 2004
Careers and Jobs in Travel and Tourism, Verité Reily Collins, 2004
Choosing Your Career, 2nd edition, Sally Longson, 2004
Great Answers to Tough Interview Questions, 7th edition, Martin Yate, 2008
Preparing the Perfect Job Application, 5th edition, Rebecca Corfield, 2009
Readymade CVs, 4th edition, Lynn Williams, 2008
Readymade Job Search Letters, 4th edition, Lynn Williams, 2008
Right Career Moves Handbook, Sophie Allen, 2005
Successful Interview Skills, 5th edition, Rebecca Corfield, 2009
Ultimate Cover Letters, 2nd edition, Martin Yate, 2008
Ultimate CV, 2nd edition, Martin Yate, 2008

Ultimate Interview, 2nd edition, Lynn Williams, 2008
Ultimate Job Search, 2nd edition, Lynn Williams, 2008

Titles in the Testing Series

The Advanced Numeracy Test Workbook, 2nd edition, Mike Bryon, 2009
Aptitude, Personality and Motivation Tests, 3rd edition, Jim Barrett, 2009
The Aptitude Test Workbook, revised edition, Jim Barrett, 2008
Graduate Psychometric Test Workbook, Mike Bryon, 2005
How to Master Personality Questionnaires, 2nd edition, Mark Parkinson, 2000
How to Master Psychometric Tests, 4th edition, Mark Parkinson, 2008
How to Pass Advanced Aptitude Tests, revised edition, Jim Barrett, 2008
How to Pass Advanced Numeracy Tests, revised edition, Mike Bryon, 2008
How to Pass the Civil Service Qualifying Tests, 3rd edition, Mike Bryon, 2007
How to Pass Graduate Psychometric Tests, 2nd edition, Mike Bryon, 2001
How to Pass the New Police Selection System, revised 2nd edition, Harry Tolley, Billy Hodge and Catherine Tolley, 2007
How to Pass Numeracy Tests, 3rd edition, Harry Tolley and Ken Thomas, 2006
How to Pass Numerical Reasoning Tests, revised edition, Heidi Smith, 2006
How to Pass Professional Level Psychometric Tests, 2nd edition, Sam Al-Jajjoka, 2004
How to Pass Selection Tests, 3rd edition, Mike Bryon and Sanjay Modha, 2005

How to Pass Technical Selection Tests, 2nd edition, Mike Bryon and Sanjay Modha, 2005

How to Pass Verbal Reasoning Tests, 3rd edition, Harry Tolley and Ken Thomas, 2006

How to Succeed at an Assessment Centre, 3rd edition, Harry Tolley and Robert Wood, 2009

IQ and Psychometric Tests, 2nd edition, Philip Carter, 2007

IQ and Psychometric Test Workbook, Philip Carter, 2005

The Numeracy Test Workbook, Mike Bryon, 2006

Test Your Own Aptitude, 3rd edition, Jim Barrett and Geoff Williams, 2003

Ultimate Psychometric Tests, Mike Bryon, 2008

CD ROMs

Psychometric Tests, Volume 1, The Times Testing Series, Editor Mike Bryon 2002

Test Your Aptitude, Volume 1, The Times Testing Series, Editor Mike Bryon, 2002

Test Your IQ, Volume 1, The Times Testing Series, Editor Mike Bryon, 2002

Index

Lightning Source UK Ltd.
Milton Keynes UK
UKOW06f1015240615

253982UK00019B/163/P